Questioning Worship

T G A BAKER

(handwritten above name: "om" "EORGE" "DAMES")

Questioning Worship

❀

SCM PRESS LTD

To my Aunt Irene

AUG 9 '77

334 02281 9

First published 1977
by SCM Press Ltd
56 Bloomsbury Street London WC1

© T. G. A. Baker 1977

Filmset by Northumberland Press Ltd, Gateshead
and printed in Great Britain
by Fletcher & Son Ltd,
Norwich

Contents

Foreword

It is really something of an impertinence for one who can make few claims to liturgical scholarship to write a book, however modest, about contemporary worship. So perhaps I may be allowed a word of explanation about how it came to be written. It originated in an article which I contributed to a volume of essays in honour of Christopher Evans, written by a number of his pupils and associates, and published by SCM Press in 1975 (*What about the New Testament?* ed. Morna Hooker and Colin Hickling). The subject of the article was liturgical revision in the light of New Testament scholarship, but it touched on a number of wider issues as well. Some people were kind enough to suggest that the questions raised in it merited rather more extensive treatment. This little book is a response to that suggestion. It is in fact an expansion of that article, set in a wider context, and with a good deal of additional material. Quite coincidentally, it was written at the same time as the whole subject was being given a good airing in the pages of the periodical *Theology*. The views here expressed were reached quite independently of that enquiry. However, the fact that they coincide so closely may be thought to be of some significance.

I would like at the outset to guard against a possible misunderstanding. The criticisms which will be levelled at some features of the new liturgies might suggest that I am opposed to the whole programme of liturgical revision. That is far from being the case. I have always supported the cause, and fully appreciate the merits of the new services. I would be sad if what I have written were to be used as ammunition by those who are campaigning for a return to the Latin mass, or the Book of Common Prayer.

Although I have tried to include references to a number of revised liturgies, some may feel that a disproportionate amount of space has been devoted to the Church of England service known as Series 3 ('The Order for Holy Communion, Alternative Services, Series 3'). This is quite simply because that service is the one with which I am most familiar, and which is used almost exclusively in the cathedral which I serve.

Many of the ideas expressed in these pages derive from informal conversations with a number of people, and especially with my friend and former colleague, Canon Robert Symonds, who was himself once a member of the Archbishops' Liturgical Commission. He will recognize in these pages some of his own insights, although I suspect that there are others which he might wish to disown. Finally I would like to record my appreciation of the efficiency with which my secretary, Mrs Jan Barnes, has helped to prepare the manuscript, and read the proofs.

Worcester
November 1976

I

Worship Today

Where we are and how we got here

Rapidity of change is not a characteristic normally associated with venerable institutions, least of all with the churches. Any bishop or archdeacon will tell you that it usually takes a quite prodigious expenditure of time and energy to effect the tiniest and most obviously necessary change in the way things are done. Always it is necessary to make haste slowly, to tarry the Lord's leisure. 'Immobilism' is the ugly word which Roman Catholics use to describe this state of affairs. Yet in one sphere, and that the least likely, the changes have been swift and dramatic. In almost every church today quite remarkable changes have taken place in public worship, within the short space of less than ten years, and against common expectation. Roman Catholics had used the same mass, and in much the same way, since the Council of Trent in the sixteenth century. Anglicans had used and valued the Book of Common Prayer since 1662. Now, within the space of a very few years, the mass has been subjected to quite radical changes, and the Book of Common Prayer has virtually been replaced by services of a different breed. The liturgical ice-age has been followed by an avalanche of new things. It is all very extra-ordinary. It seems only the day before yesterday that Roman Catholics pointed to the traditional mass, celebrated in the time honoured fashion and with all its atmosphere of mystery, as one of their greatest assets over protestant worship. Many non-believers have agreed with this assessment from the touch line. It seems only yesterday that Anglican clergymen and apologists were speaking about 'our incomparable prayer book'. Today both Tridentine mass and 1662 prayer book are swiftly being relegated to the limbo of ecclesiastical antiquities.

Changes in the forms of services have been accompanied by equally swift and dramatic changes in the way those services are conducted. Not much more than ten years or so ago the priest who celebrated the eucharist facing the people was thought to be rather eccentric. Today this position is almost universal in Roman Catholic churches, and very common elsewhere. The baroque splendours of Roman Catholic and high Anglican worship have (except in a few Anglo-catholic ghettoes) given way to a ceremonial which is either austere in its simplicity, or matey in its informality, or a mixture of both. Elaborate and in some cases finely constructed high altars are left to rot, while a simple table in the main body of the church is used instead. The people stand to pray and rarely kneel; often the seating arrangements make such a posture impossible anyway. The music is usually congregational throughout, and there is sometimes a congregational choir practice before the service begins. Lay people, and sometimes children, read the lessons and conduct the intercessions. It is all a very far cry from solemn High Mass, or for that matter stately Sung Mattins.

Now such a sudden revolution could not have happened unless there had been considerable pressure behind it, a good deal of enthusiasm somewhere, and some great expectations. We are not surprised to learn then that, though the changes happened suddenly, they came as the climax of a movement which had been going on quietly for some time previously. This is known as the Liturgical Movement, and some brief account of it must be given before we continue with these reflections.

The movement originated in the Roman Catholic Church, its birth place being the Benedictine Abbey of Solesme in the years following its refounding in 1832. At this stage it was dominated by a scholarly interest in the origins and history of the liturgy. Later it broadened out into a more practical and pastoral concern to 'bring the liturgy to life'. In the first decade of this century Pope Pius X called for a more active participation of the laity in the liturgy as a means of spiritual renewal, and for a more frequent reception of holy communion at the mass. In 1909 a catholic conference at Malines put great emphasis on the liturgy as a means of instruction, and as the living centre of the church's mission in the world. The Liturgical Movement thus became associated with the incarnational theology so characteristic of the early twentieth century, a theology which spoke of the sanctification of all human life and endeavour. 'Christ the Lord of all life' became its slogan in some quarters. It also came to be associated with a renewed interest in biblical theology, and in particular with such biblical images as the Body of Christ and the People of God. At this stage then there was a promising interaction between theologians, biblical exegetes, liturgical scholars and the pastors of the church. Interest in discovering the origins of liturgy went hand in hand with a practical concern about the present needs and opportunities of the contemporary church. In spite of a good deal of opposition on the part of the traditionalists its influence spread from France to Belgium and Germany, and reached the USA. Its effect came to be felt in the way the liturgy was conducted in a few parish churches and monasteries, especially in northern Europe. In 1947 Pope Pius XII devoted a whole encyclical to it, thus giving the movement official recognition at the highest possible level. The first actual and official changes in the liturgy itself took place in 1951 when the liturgy for the Paschal Vigil on the night of Holy Saturday was restored. Five years later the whole of the Holy Week observances were drastically reformed.

All this, of course, was but part of the general ferment taking place in the Roman Catholic Church, a ferment culminating in the calling of the Second Vatican Council. The first of the Constitutions to be published by the Council was *De Sacra Liturgia*, which was promulgated by the Pope in December 1963. It was a clear statement of the theology and purpose of the liturgy, showed a keen awareness of the present pastoral and evangelistic needs of the church, and opened the way to the use of the vernacular in place of Latin. The implementation of the recommendations and principles of the Constitution was swift, and will be discussed a little later in this chapter.

Before that we must look to see what was going on in Britain at this time. For, though the influence of the movement in the Roman Catholic Church spread widely on the continent, it was slow to influence its life here. This no doubt was due to the fact that English Catholicism represented a minority church seeking to establish and maintain its strength in what had until recently, partly as a result of the cult of the English martyrs, been regarded

3

as an alien and indeed hostile environment. Hence it continued to be somewhat insular, and resistant to any change which might seem to be selling the pass to protestantism. The Liturgical Movement initially found an entry into Britain chiefly by way of the Church of England itself. The work of Roman Catholic liturgical scholars was taken up in Britain by such Anglican liturgiologists as E. C. Ratcliffe, Dom Gregory Dix, A. Couratin and J. G. Davies. At the same time the principles and practices of the Liturgical Movement, for the time being by-passing the Roman Catholic Church, quickly influenced Anglican church life, especially under the initial impact of the work and writings of Fr Gabriel Hebert SSM. It swiftly replaced non-communicating Sung Eucharist and 11 o'clock Mattins with the 9.30 a.m. Parish Communion in parish after parish. It was given impetus by the publication in 1935 of Hebert's highly influential book *Liturgy and Society*. What makes this a great work, however dated in some respects, is its concern to relate liturgy to the social and economic aspects of the human condition, and to provide reflections on its expression in art, architecture and music. Its sub-title 'The Function of the Church in the Modern World' well expresses the breadth of its scope and vision. It had to do with the world. Hebert taught that 'if Christianity is the redemption of all life, the things done and said in church must have a direct relation to the things done and said everywhere else; the sacraments and the liturgy exist in order to give to human life its true direction in relation to God, and to bind men in fellowship with one another'.[1] His teaching on the offertory, understood as the offering of the whole creation symbolized in the oblation of bread and cup, reflected the incarnational theology of his day. So too his teaching on the eucharist as the sacramental expression of the fellowship and mission of the church reflected the contemporary re-discovery of New Testament theology concerning the church as the People of God. As in the writings of Roman Catholic scholars we find a real attempt to relate the principles and practices of liturgy to the positive insights of current theological thought.

Liturgy and Society was followed by the publication of a series of essays, edited by the same Fr Hebert, called *The Parish Communion* (SPCK 1937). The essayists aimed to commend the celebration of holy communion, with general communion of the

4

people, as the main service of Sunday, followed by a shared breakfast, and later in the week by a regular meeting of the worshipping congregation. Their aims and ideals, at least in externals, met with wide acceptance. A special new movement called 'Parish and People' was inaugurated in order to facilitate the process of change. The pattern of Sunday worship in many parishes was changed almost beyond recognition. *Yet*, all the time the old prayer book of 1662 continued to be used, though with varying degrees of loyalty. Many parishes which were influenced by the Parish and People movement did not wish it otherwise. Many continued to value this ancient rite very highly, considering it to be a very suitable vehicle, when sensitively handled, for the new ideas and principles. Some even continued to speak of it as 'our incomparable liturgy'. But others were discontented with it, and longed for a rite which would convey more directly the essential meaning of the eucharist, and one which would be at once more modern and more primitive in form and content. The future was to lie with these more radical reformers.

So we come to the re-writing of liturgies which has happened so swiftly over the past few years. In the Roman Catholic Church it was accomplished by authoritative decree, at the now proverbial stroke. Roman Catholics who had been used all their life to the Tridentine mass in Latin woke one morning to a brand new mass, very much simplified, recited in the vernacular, with four possible versions of the canon (the central eucharistic prayer), and with the whole of the first part of the service conducted from a lectern rather than the altar. The new mass was obligatory, the old one to be used only on special occasions and with special permission. The fussy ceremonial was reduced to a minimum of special postures and gestures. The priest normally faced the people across an altar table set in the midst of the church. This quickly resulted in great changes in the architecture of new churches, and the furnishings of existing ones. The new puritanism and informality of Roman Catholic worship is now almost universal. It is to be found in the remotest Sicilian village just as much as in the most avant-garde of Netherland parishes. It is true that for a time both priest and people had to make do with a plethora of little booklets, or even duplicated sheets of paper, while the changes were working through. But now there are beautifully printed missals setting out the new services in some detail and with careful explanatory notes. And the clergy have in the newly published *Divine Office* a finely produced prayer book for all occasions, which, if bulky and expensive, is already the envy of many non-Roman priests who are floundering still in a sea of experimental services. Amongst Roman Catholics the exercise appears to be complete already; and British Catholicism has, by and large, caught up with the rest of the Catholic world.

In the Church of England the process has been somewhat more gentle, and not so complete. This has been due in part to the comprehensiveness of that church, a factor which makes unanimity in liturgical revision a great deal harder to achieve. It has been due in part to the State connection; until quite recently every deviation from the 1662 Book of Common Prayer and every experimental service apart from it needed the consent of parliament, with all the red tape which went with it. And it has been due in part to the less authoritarian character of the Church of England and its rather different way of doing things. The process was initiated by the setting up in 1954 of a Liturgical Commission, which produced a series of new services of all kinds. But each had to be debated and approved by the Church Assembly, later the General Synod. This was a lengthy and sometimes hilarious procedure. Even then they were offered to the parishes only as temporary and experimental services needing the consent of the Parochial Church Council before use. The Book of Common Prayer remained, and still remains, the official service book of the Church of England, and continues to be used in many places. But these very facts make it all the more remarkable that, in the space of a few years the new services, and the new ways of conducting them, have spread like a prairie fire, and that the Book of Common Prayer is used in an ever decreasing number of parishes. It is interesting to note that the fairly radical revision of the communion office known as Series 2 was produced by the Commission in the first place as an appendix to another production, and in a very rough and ready fashion. This was because its members expected it to be used over a quite long experimental period in just a few rather daring and progressive parishes. Against all expectation it caught on extremely rapidly and soon became firmly established in perhaps the majority of Anglican parishes. The revisers were caught out by the speed of their success. Indeed so firmly did it establish itself that many church people forgot that it was intended only as an aperitif to whet the appetite for something more nourishing. That is why its more polished and carefully constructed successor called Series 3 (which incidentally used the pronoun 'you' instead of 'thou' as an address to God) has not made its way so easily. Even so there are indications that it is the more radical Series 3 which will ultimately prevail.

It would be possible to trace the development in other churches, and in such communities as Taizé and Iona. But this book is not intended to be a comprehensive survey of liturgical development. Already the reader may feel that I have more than sufficiently laboured the point that the development has been remarkably swift. I have done so at the risk of boring you because I want to highlight the equally remarkable fact that *a sense of disappointment and dissatisfaction has followed just as rapidly*. There have indeed been great expectations. In one sense those expectations have been fulfilled more completely and rapidly than seemed possible in one's wildest dreams. In another and broader sense they have been disappointed, and already there is some disillusion.

Let there be no doubt about the keenness of those expectations, or of the early enthusiasm. One remembers the eagerness with which the Parish Communion was introduced into parish after parish and the sense of renewal which it certainly engendered. One remembers the excitement which greeted the publication of such books as Dom Gregory Dix's *The Shape of the Liturgy* (Dacre Press 1945). One remembers too the sense of liberation with which many Roman Catholic clergy greeted the reform of the missal and the breviary. I myself remember the excitement with which my colleagues and I at Wells Theological College sought to introduce the students to the new principles of worship, and to break down some of the stuffiness of the old.

Now, only ten years on, these principles have been widely accepted, and are now enshrined in official new rites. And already there is disenchantment. Of course we must allow for the fact that the initial enthusiasm accompanying any new movement is bound to wane, especially as the new principles become institutionalized.

7

But this factor is not enough to explain the sense of disappointment. Somehow the liturgy has not 'come to life' quite in the way we had hoped. It would be unfair and unreasonable to attribute the present decline in churchgoing to the new forms of worship. This is part and parcel of a much more general decline in institutional religion, and has much deeper roots. But it is perhaps significant that the new forms have failed to bring as much fresh vitality to the worship of existing congregations as might have been hoped. It is also significant that liturgical reform has been largely a clerical pursuit. The laity have been generally content to go along with it, but with a comparative lack of enthusiasm. With them it has been a matter of two cheers, or perhaps even only one, for the new forms. The great mass of the people who rarely darken the door of a church have been affected not at all.

Even more significant to my mind is the fact that for the most part people do not *enjoy* going to church as much as once they did. Do I? Do you? Some magic seems to have departed. I know that I shall be told rather solemnly that one goes to church to give and not simply to get. But I would submit that there is something gravely wrong with worship which somehow disappoints expectations, and to which one goes mainly out of a sense of duty.

So we have the paradox. On the one hand we see a revolution in liturgy carried out with surprising speed; enormous enthusiasm at least from the clergy; the attaining in a short time of all the aims and objects of the early reformers; great expectations of a liturgy coming to life. On the other hand we detect a vague sense of unease, of disappointment, of hopes unfilled. There is little doubt that many people feel that the new services are worthy, but in some ways unsatisfying. Others feel, whether consciously or subconsciously, that while solving some problems the new forms raise a number of others. The purpose of this book is to reflect on this paradox. It will not delve deep into liturgical scholarship. Nor will it attempt to deal with the much deeper and wider issues which have to do with the spiritual crises of our times. It will confine itself to the narrower front of liturgical reform. On the other hand it will attempt to show that some of the reasons for our liturgical discontents have deep roots in *theology*, and to suggest that this aspect of the matter has received far too little attention either in the works of liturgical scholars or in popular writings and commentaries.

But first there ought to be some attempt to examine gains and losses, to draw up a credit and debit balance sheet. Liturgical renewal has long been overdue, and its sheer inevitability constitutes an important factor in its assessment. The relative disappointment of certain hopes does not mean that those hopes were misplaced, or that nothing has been accomplished partially to fulfil them.

2

Gains and Losses

The advantages of recent liturgical change have often been rehearsed. The fact that some enthusiasts have claimed too much should not be allowed to blind us to the very substantial gains that have been achieved. So, at the risk of treading well worn paths, it is necessary for the sake of balance to list those gains at this point. Some were deliberately intended, some are by-products. We will deal first with the direct gains to put on the credit side of the balance sheet.

1. Liturgical change has undoubtedly resulted in the sweeping away of a great deal of suffocating formalism and fussiness in worship. When one reflects on the way in which for generations Roman Catholics have been subjected to mumbled masses, stiff with formalism, perfunctorily performed, and celebrated as if the congregation did not exist, then it is hardly surprising that some at least have found in the new services a great liberation of spirit. It is also easy to understand why so many Anglicans, who have endured for so long the cold, tedious and convention-ridden worship of full-scale Mattins, have greeted some aspects of the new forms of worship with relief. The inhibited and demure demeanour with which much conventional worship has been conducted has taken a salutory knock.

At a more theological level, the new patterns of worship have reflected the recently renewed emphasis on the immanence of God, the replacement of the distant potentate by the God of the here and now, of the 'disposer supreme' by the 'beyond in the midst'. I shall in fact argue in a later chapter that this emphasis has received all too little expression in the actual *words* of the new rites, but it is certainly reflected in the new church furnishings and the more homely ceremonial. This too makes for a more informal, more human and humanizing type of worship. So does the greater emphasis on the notes of joy, celebration, resurrection and hope. The Roman mass is no longer so exclusively a propitiatory sacrifice offered for the sins of the living and the dead. Cranmer's guilt-ridden liturgy, with its almost exclusive emphasis on the all-sufficient atoning death of Christ, and its funereal conception of memorial, has been replaced by a rite which, like the authors of the New Testament literature, views everything in the light of resurrection.

2. Another beneficial result of liturgical change has been an increased degree of lay participation. The point needs no labouring, but is of vital importance. In the old days Roman Catholic mass tended to be an external spectacle, a kind of 'tableau vivant' played before an audience which took virtually no part. The 1662 communion office was even more a clerically dominated affair, a lengthy monologue on the part of the minister, with next to no opportunities for the people to express their fellowship one with another. The great increase in lay participation found in the new services has made possible a fresh understanding of the corporate and social quality of church membership. This in its turn has opened up the fresh understanding of man as essentially a social being, and therefore of the church's vocation to concern itself with man in society and not exclusively with men as individuals. It is perhaps not a coincidence that the new and unaccustomed concern with social involvement to be found amongst some conservative evangelicals has been accompanied by their equally unexpected acceptance of liturgical revision.

3. The provision of services in genuinely contemporary English must be accounted a real gain, in spite of some unfortunate side effects which will be considered later. This after all is simply doing for our own generation what Cranmer attempted to do for his. The inevitable result of using 'thou' instead of 'you' when praying to God is to produce what has been called a 'church diction' not really consonant with the living language of the twentieth century. It has resulted in the unhappy 'mock-gothic' style which mars so many of the semi-official collections of prayers still currently in use in many churches. The change to modern English has begun to discredit styles which are simply imitative of the past. It has also produced the beneficial by-

product of encouraging an openness to contemporary design in church furnishings and ornaments. I am referring not only to churches, like the new Roman Catholic cathedrals at Liverpool and Bristol, which have been deliberately built in modern styles, but also to the fact that it is no longer considered necessary to use only imitative designs for new furnishings in mediaeval buildings. A genuinely contemporary altar frontal set against the background of an early English quire and a Victorian reredos is now seen as an enrichment and not an anomaly. It all contributes to a sense of the livingness of the church.

4. Current liturgical revision has drawn very creatively on the meticulous and rigorous standards of first-rate liturgical scholars from all traditions. These scholars have discovered a great wealth of new data about the origins and early history of the liturgy which were unknown to an earlier generation of revisers, to say nothing of Cranmer and the other compilers of the Book of Common Prayer. They have brought fresh insights to liturgical theory and practice which introduce a new factor into the sterile controversies born of the Reformation period, and thus help to transcend them. Conversely it could be said that the practical interest in contemporary reform has served to give a great impetus to critical research into the origins and development of liturgy, from which we have learned much. There has been a two-way traffic which has proved fruitful.

5. One of the results of this liturgical research has been to bring into clearer focus the heart of the eucharist as something done not said, and to draw attention to what Gregory Dix has called its 'four-fold shape': 'For in the night in which he was betrayed he *took* bread; and when he had *given thanks* to thee, he *broke* it, and *gave* it to his disciples.' In the Tridentine mass this 'shape' was blurred by a great deal of extremely repetitious material. In the prayer book communion office it was badly obscured by the intrusion of a great deal of intercessory and penitential material. The clear exposure of the eucharist as essentially *symbolic action* has been most helpful to those who have a basically Christian outlook on life, and who wish to associate themselves with the church, but for whom assent to certain credal propositions present severe intellectual difficulties.

6. In some quarters at least the renewed interest in relevant

liturgy has stimulated the will to mission. The corporate character of eucharistic worship, and the emphasis on the material elements used in it, has contributed towards a lively debate concerning the connection between worship and mission, and called in question the idea of worship as essentially a withdrawal from the world and the pressures of everyday life. Whether or not one agrees with all his conclusions, none has done more than Dr J. G. Davies, in his many writings, to foster this debate.

So far we have spoken of the direct and intended results of liturgical revision. Now we must mention two important by-products to set on the credit side of the balance.

It has made a most significant contribution to the cause of Christian unity, and to ecumenical understanding. This has been due partly to the fact that its scholars have belonged to many different traditions, and have worked together without party bias or denominational axes to grind. This has fostered a great respect for impartial scholarship in this field, leading to a real desire to recover or discover principles of common worship which will serve the whole church and not just one branch of it.

It is remarkable that the revised eucharistic rites of most of the major churches of the west are so very similar both in their structure and often in their wording as well. No longer is it possible to make such a disagreeably hard and fast distinction between the 'Mass' and the 'Lord's Supper'. Christians from different traditions may now attend each other's eucharists and recognize them as the same service. The 'missa normativa' as celebrated at St Sulpice in Paris is difficult to distinguish from the Series 3 Sung Eucharist in Worcester Cathedral. This growing together of the churches in common worship has recently received a great impetus through the publication by the International Consultation on English Texts of a set of new texts for use by Christians of all denominations in the English speaking world. These are now available in a booklet entitled *Prayers we have in common* (Chapman 1971), and comprise all the sung portions of the eucharist together with the Lord's Prayer. These texts are now in use amongst Roman Catholics, and have been adopted by a number of provinces within the Anglican communion, and by a number of Reformed churches.

We have noted that the Church of England presents special

problems because of its wide variation of churchmanship. Yet here too liturgical change has in practice had a unifying effect. This process began with the introduction of the Parish Communion as the main act of Sunday worship, thus breaking down the polarization of Mattins and Sung Eucharist parishes. It was further advanced by the publication of Series 2 and Series 3, both of which have proved acceptable to Anglicans of widely different churchmanship. The simplification of ceremonial has produced similar results. It is no longer so easy to categorize Anglican parishes as 'high' or 'low'. At residential conferences for clergy it is no longer so necessary in the interests of fair shares to have a 'high' day and a 'low' day. The same rite, the same dress, and very similar ceremonial will do every day, and nobody is offended. I am sure that the cathedral which I serve is not the only one where it has been found possible to devise a rite, ceremonial and form of clergy apparel which is equally acceptable to all the canons concerned, in spite of their widely divergent churchmanship and theological positions. Nor is this based on compromise, but rather on the replacement of the old divisions by something genuinely new which can transcend them. In particular, the peculiarly divisive theology of a 'moment' of consecration, with the ceremonial which used to accompany it, is being replaced by a theology which understands consecration in terms of the eucharistic action as a whole, without the need to emphasize any particular 'moment' within it.

Alongside the good ecumenical by-products of the Liturgical Movement one should set the opportunity which it has opened up for the spiritual and theological education of the laity, and indeed of the clergy too. The need to introduce congregations to the new forms of worship has made it possible for them to enter more intelligently into that worship, to be much more sensitive to its spiritual potential, and to make it much more their own. More importantly this exercise has been the means of acquainting them with spiritual and theological issues of which they may have been wholly or partly unaware. Liturgy can be a gateway to Christian maturity and understanding. The tragedy is that these opportunities have so often been missed. Either the changes have been thrust upon a recalcitrant and mystified congregation without proper preparation or consultation. Or else this preparation has been too exclusively centred on the externals of liturgy rather than on its deeper spiritual and theological implications. Nevertheless the opportunity is there, and in some places has been used to good effect. So that is gain.

So much for the credit side. The reader may wish to add to the list. What should be in the debit column? I suggest four main items. The first three will be set down summarily at this point and will be developed in later chapters. The fourth we will deal with at somewhat greater length.

1. The first concerns the use of scripture in the new rites. It will be argued that almost all the vital issues raised by post-critical biblical scholarship, especially on the New Testament, have been by-passed or evaded. The insights of such scholarship have been largely ignored. The problems raised by it have been not only ignored but in some cases aggravated. It will be further argued that the new rites offer altogether too heavy a biblical diet, and foster the kind of biblicism which, however popular at the moment, is neither true to the spirit of the scriptures themselves nor of lasting relevance to the contemporary situation or to the future. To many this assessment will appear exceptionally perverse, because time and again the new services have been commended precisely on the ground of their biblical basis and content. It will need therefore further defence and justification.

2. In similar fashion the new rites have for the most part by-passed or evaded the issues raised by recent and contemporary theology. It is as if the great giants of nineteenth and twentieth century theology had never existed, as if the tremendous theological ferment in the church during this period had never happened. Again the positive insights have been ignored, and the problems either dodged or even aggravated. This too is a sweeping and perhaps surprising judgment which will need a separate chapter to explain and justify.

3. The next criticism is less surprising, has often been voiced, and will no doubt sound echoing chords in the minds of many of my readers. I refer to the comparative loss of what is often called the 'sense of the numinous', but which I would rather refer to as aesthetic, emotional and spiritual impoverishment. There is a certain dullness and drabness about the new services, and the way they are often presented. Their admirable informality easily

degenerates into a wholly unadmirable superficiality, or even gimmickry. Although this criticism is more widely accepted, it raises a variety of issues which again deserve a chapter to themselves.

4. The fourth problem raised by current trends in public worship is more far reaching and concerns the relation of Christianity to the life and culture of the nation. The intention of the early liturgical reformers was to 'bring the liturgy to life', to make it more approachable by the common man, and a more suitable vehicle for expressing the personal, social and political dimensions of faith. In practice it has often had the reverse effect. It has tended to make church people rather inward looking, more bothered about the correct place for the 'Pax' than about the plight of the homeless, the underprivileged, the oppressed and the starving, and the spiritual needs of individuals. Far too much time has been spent in synods and conferences on revising the liturgy, far too little on wrestling with the current crisis of faith and understanding, or with the great moral dilemmas of life in modern society – education, housing, automation, unemployment, class and race conflict, to mention but a few. It is possible to become just as preoccupied with the niceties of ritual and ceremonial in the modern forms of worship as in the older patterns. The cult of simplicity can be just as obsessive as the delight in intricate and elaborate ceremonial. The 'sanctuary slug' is to be found on both soils. There can be little doubt that concern for liturgical change has contributed to the increasingly ghetto mentality of many congregations, and to the widening of the gulf between Christianity and the mainstream of national life.

The growing centrality of the eucharist and the emphasis on frequent communion has tended to have the same effect, the exact opposite of what was intended. Gordon Dunstan, in a *Theology* editorial, made a point which has some validity in spite of the somewhat extreme way it is expressed: 'The cultural alienation of the Church of England from the national life has anticipated the legal separation. Its habits of parochial worship are now widely those of a eucharistic sect self-conscious in fellowship and in its good works. Its repertory is being reduced to Series X with everything, like chips in the canteen cafeteria. Mattins and Evensong are being forced out, and what we may call the

16

Englishman's natural Christianity with them ... Today these men are alienated, left without link with the Church which offers them a family Communion or nothing...'[1] It is interesting that Trevor Beeson, himself something of a radical, and from a standpoint in many ways far removed from the traditionalism of Gordan Dunstan, can write as follows: '... five centuries of continuous use have served to burn something of the thought and language of the Prayer Book into the corporate memory of the English nation. When the words are those of the most creative era in English language and literature, the evocative effects are often deeper than is commonly realised ... those who come to the Church of England on the occasion of a Baptism, a Marriage or a Burial ... find that the words and phrases of the Book of Common Prayer ring bells of one kind or another in their consciousness. What this amounts to in terms of spirituality and insight is obviously impossible to tell. It may be no more than sentiment, or vague folk memory. But something so intangible, yet so common, cannot lightly be dismissed or cast aside, least of all by a church which still claims to represent in some sense the spiritual dimension of the English nation as a whole.'[2] It is in this connection that one cannot but regret the fact that there is no longer a Prayer Book which one can keep in one's home, or give as a confirmation present to one's godchild; that there is no longer a single version of the Bible from which memorable and evocative quotations can be made; no longer one version of the Lord's Prayer familiar to all. Even when the salutation 'The Lord be with you' is made, the reply tends to be a jumbled confusion of 'And with thy spirit' and 'And also with you'! These things are perhaps inevitable at a time of transition, but that a real loss is involved can hardly be doubted.

Nor is it only the 'ordinary man' or the occasional church-goer who tends to be confused or even alienated by these changes. There are also the 'loners' – the temperamentally ungregarious; the people who walk softly through life; the folk whose capacity to influence affairs is slight; the people whose secular responsibilities are too heavy to allow much time for church affairs; those who are by nature contemplative; the modern counterparts of those who of old followed the ancient eremitic vocation. It is hard for such folk to be offered nothing but an extremely matey and noisy family communion, harder still when they are made to feel guilty about not enjoying it. It is all too easy to despise those who insist on preferring the 'quiet eight o'clock', for amongst their numbers is to be found some deeply spiritual and devoted people who radiate the peace and compassion of Christ wherever they go. The little old lady who creeps into the eight o'clock communion, and then creeps out again before anybody can speak to her, may not contribute much to the external fellowship of Christians, but she may be a power house of interior prayer and loving intercession. The Christian businessman or politician, burdened with the heavy weight of grave decisions affecting the lives and livelihoods of many, looks to the Sunday worship primarily for inner, spiritual refreshment. This is not in any way to deny what has been said earlier about the advantages of greater lay participation in worship and mission, for the people to whom I refer are a minority group. But minorities should be catered for, not forced to conform. At present all that is offered them by way of refreshment in public worship is the said communion, or cathedral evensong, both of them commodities not always within easy reach.

Nor should it be forgotten that liturgical revision has been for the most part a clerical preoccupation. So great has been the interest among the clergy that in some cases it has amounted to a kind of self-indulgence. Changes have been introduced for no better reason than that the parson likes it that way. He forgets that the people do not always share his own enthusiasm. He is for ever making fussy little changes in the rites and ceremonial, constantly engaged in experiments carried out in an insensitive and self-centred way. In the editorial already referred to, Gordon Dunstan writes: 'Woe to the shepherds who feed themselves and not the flock; and the clergy *have* fed themselves, indulged their own liturgical addictions to an inordinate degree. For a year or two, they satisfy the more clericalized of their flock: but the staleness will sicken when surely, and soon, it comes.' The condemnation is too sweeping, but it contains more than a grain of truth.

Such, briefly, is the tally of gain and loss, debit and credit. A large part of the chapters which follow will concentrate on the debit column, and therefore will be critical in tone. The reader is asked, however, to remember the very real gains that have been

18

achieved and which have been rehearsed in the earlier part of this chapter; and also to bear in mind that it is not my purpose to suggest that we can ever simply turn the clock back and revert to the old ways. We cannot go back. But we *do* need to go forward, for reasons which we shall now consider.

3

Worship and the Bible

The idea that the revision of the liturgy is simply a matter of modernizing language is obviously superficial. It is concerned much more fundamentally with adapting it to changed circumstances, fresh ways of thought, new challenges and opportunities. Now it is a fact not to be denied that one of the most fundamental changes to have come over Christianity in recent years (at least in the West) has been a radically new approach to the scriptures, resulting from the work of biblical scholars over the last two centuries. Their painstaking application to the biblical texts of the best methods of modern historical study, coinciding as it has with great new advances in the realms of physics, biology and the behavioural sciences, have produced a sea change in the way the Bible is used and interpreted. Even those who resist these developments are affected by them, perhaps without quite knowing that they are. It is therefore reasonable to expect that the revision of the liturgy should duly reflect such a remarkable change.

Before going further along this line an important caveat must be entered. Liturgy has a strong element of conservatism built into it. Its purpose is to celebrate the most cherished and central traditions of a society, to express the experiences and convictions which its members hold in common, and to communicate those living symbols which give that society its cohesion and continuity. Therefore liturgy is resistant to passing fashions of thought, experience and expression. Now it cannot be denied that modern biblical studies are subject to such passing fashions. The conclusions of the scholars are often tentative, subject to further revision. We are therefore not surprised to find that their influence on liturgical revision is not direct and immediate. Indeed we may be grateful that this is the case. It would not be nice to be saddled with a liturgy or lectionary unduly influenced by the rather sentimentalizing 'Life of Jesus' theologies characteristic of some New Testament scholars of the turn of the century, nor by the inevitably partial understanding of the work of particular scholars such as Bultmann, Barth, Jeremias or any other of the giants. This is in no way to deny the value of all the varied phases of biblical studies, but merely to recognize that their premature petrifaction into a liturgy or lectionary would constitute a severe impoverishment of worship.

Having granted all this, however, and having made full allowance for the provisional nature of particular theories or conclusions in biblical studies, it remains true that the methods of such modern study remain fairly constant, that the use of these methods has had a very profound and lasting effect on the way the Bible is used and interpreted, and that it has led to some quite fundamental changes in theological perspective.

In the first place, it is generally recognized that every statement and every narrative in the Bible has to be understood, first of all, within its own historical setting, having due regard to its cultural milieu, to the way people then used to think about the world (very differently from the way we now think), to the kind of imagery they found meaningful (again very different from our own imagery, such as it is), and to the religious and cultural influences to which they were exposed.[1] It is equally important to have regard to the literary form in which each various section of the Bible is set. Within its pages there is a rich mixture of historical narrative, legendary embroidery, poetry, saga, myth – and it is vital to interpret each genre of literature in its own terms. It is a very wooden kind of literalism which interprets poetry as if it were prose. How much unnecessary ink has been spilt trying to prove that there once existed certain kinds of whales with mouths big enough to swallow Jonah whole, or that there was once some kind of astronomical phenomenon which can explain the extraordinary behaviour of the star which led the Wise Men to Bethlehem. It follows that the religious experience of the biblical writers is so closely bound up with their own imagery and way of putting things that it cannot be easily detached and applied direct to our own times. Neither the words nor the imagery are exempt from human limitation or error. No longer is it possible to treat the

Bible as a source book from which to gather a collection of inerrant propositions, divinely guaranteed as of timeless and universal validity.

Another important conclusion of modern study is that there is in the Bible a considerably greater variety of thought, experience and doctrine than had formerly been realized. Thus in the first three gospels we are presented with three highly distinctive portraits of Jesus and his work, which cannot be harmonized without reducing them to a shapeless pulp. Each evangelist has interpreted his material in very specific ways, and with definite ends in view. There are genuine differences in theological outlook between Paul and the author of Luke–Acts, or between Mark and Matthew. There are real differences between New Testament authors on the place of Law in Christian life, and the right relations between the Christian community and the State. It can be safely said that most of the points of controversy in the church today are reflected within the pages of the New Testament itself. This important insight calls into question the practice of quoting texts in total isolation from their setting, still more of interpreting one text by reference to another from quite another context.

It is now generally recognized that all the biblical books, in greater or lesser degree, spring out of the community life of the church (the Old Israel and the New), and often have a complicated history of development behind them. The first five books of the Old Testament were not written down by Moses. They are the end product of several centuries of the religious life of Israel, in which older elements have been subject to constant adaptation and re-editing in the light of changing ideas and circumstances, and whose final attribution to Moses must be accounted a pious fiction. They are essentially community productions. The same is true, on a smaller scale, of the first three (synoptic) gospels. These can no longer be regarded as direct eye-witness reportage of the words and deeds of Jesus. They are rather a compilation of a number of originally independent narratives, each of which shows clear traces of having been shaped and adapted, first in the period of oral transmission by early teachers and prophets, and then by the editorial work of each gospel writer. That is why we have not one but two versions of the Lord's Prayer, and why some of the parables are interpreted rather differently from one gospel to another. It seems too that these early teachers and writers were concerned not so much with providing what we would call an accurate account of 'what actually happened', but rather to relate what they had learned to the changing practical and religious needs and problems of the community which they served. What may loosely be called 'fact' and 'interpretation' have become so closely interwoven that it is difficult to distinguish one from the other. As for the gospel of John, it is generally agreed that, however much genuine reminiscence may underlie the account, the words attributed to Jesus are not the words which he used, but the meditations and reflections of the evangelist struggling to translate an earlier form of Christian teaching into terms more deeply meaningful to himself and his readers. Even in the New Testament epistles we are constantly coming across fragments of hymns, catechetical instruction and credal formulae, which have taken shape in the community life of the church long before the writer put pen to paper.

It follows that it is no longer possible to draw a very hard and fast distinction between scripture and tradition, between the authority of what is in the Bible and what is not. The point is put in an article by Professor C. F. Evans with characteristic sharpness: 'The Bible is now as it were open at both ends. Emerging from a mist of legend at one end, departing in a haze of apostolic pseudonymity at the other, the canon of scripture can hardly be taken by us with the deadly seriousness with which our forefathers have taken it.'[2] It is now seen that the New Testament is the deposit at a particular period of time of a stream of living tradition which was already flowing before the books came to be written, and which continued to flow uninterruptedly after they were written.

Now in view of the conservative bias endemic in public liturgy already alluded to in this chapter, it is not to be expected that these developments in our understanding of the Bible, comparatively recent as they are, should make any immediate or dramatic impact upon it. On the other hand, when we recognize the profound changes which these developments have wrought upon theological method in general, and on scriptural interpretation in particular, one might reasonably have hoped that they would have had *some* influence on liturgical revision. What do we find? Well, there are a few traces of such an influence here and there. For example, in the older lectionaries, up to and including the 1922 lectionary for the Anglican daily office (taken over, with some revisions, in the Prayer Book as Proposed in 1928), the readings from the four gospels were often conflated together in a harmonizing fashion. More recent revisions of the lectionary prescribe the reading of each gospel in turn, and in more digestible portions. In the new Calendar and Lectionary adopted by the Church of England Liturgical Commission, and also in that now in use in the Roman Catholic Church, there is a much wider choice of readings at the eucharist, following a two year or three year cycle, and with some thematic connection between the readings. We also find certain signs that recent New Testament scholarship on the eschatological mould of New Testament language and thought has had some effect. Thus in the Lord's Prayer the moralistic and unbiblical translation 'lead us not into temptation' has been replaced by the phrase 'do not bring us to the time of trial' i.e. the time of severe testing and persecution associated in much New Testament thought with the birth pangs of the new age of God's final victory. The wording of the eucharistic prayer in most revisions has certainly been influenced by recent research into the strong connotations in Jewish thought of the word 'anamnesis' (memorial), whereby that which is remembered (the Exodus in Jewish worship, the Christ Event in Christian liturgy) is thought of as being realized afresh in the present, rather than simply imagined or recollected as a thing of the past.

There are also some traces of a more subtle kind. For example in the recent new Order of Worship put out by the United Reformed Church in 1974, the narrative of the institution of the Lord's Supper is introduced by the words 'Hear the narrative of the institution of the Lord's Supper as it was recorded by the apostle Paul.' Such a cautiously worded statement may well reflect an understanding that there are other and different narratives of the same event in the New Testament, and that scholars agree that it is difficult to be at all certain of the precise words or intentions of Jesus in the Upper Room.

At this point the reader may well feel that I am scraping the bottom of the barrel, and he would be right. The sad truth is that the influence of New Testament scholarship on the liturgy has been marginal. Perhaps it would be more accurate to say that, through insensitivity of treatment, the insights which it offers have been obscured and the problems it raises aggravated. We may look at this under four heads.

1. As we have seen, the general tendency of biblical studies has been to emphasize the community origin of most of the writings, to blur the distinction between scripture and tradition, and to call in question the notion of the Bible as a 'holy book' hermetically sealed at both ends, with a quite independent authority, and a meaning clearly intelligible and of direct, indeed timeless application. The Roman Catholic Church has never given to the Bible such a unique authority, and even before the advent of modern scholarship the Church of England has appealed to tradition and reason as necessary adjuncts to the authority of scripture. Yet almost all the revised rites are more heavily and exclusively biblical than their predecessors. In Series 3, for example, there are now three biblical lessons instead of only two; and the rubrics allow and indeed encourage a psalm and/or a canticle (almost always biblical) in no less than three places. Unless the service is to become intolerably long, this means a curtailment of time for hymns and the sermon. The fact that the sermon now follows immediately after the biblical readings (often provided with a theme) tends to force it into a strictly biblical mould just at a time when many preachers are finding it more helpful to preach more directly on issues of immediate concern to their congregations without the restriction of particular texts or allusions. There is irony in the fact that, at a time when straight expository preaching is proving less effective than before, the structure of the new liturgies should tend to force the sermon into this kind of strait jacket. It is a further irony that, at a time when the Bible is advisedly being given a less exclusive place in Religious Education syllabuses, the liturgy is becoming more exclusively biblical than ever before. One can understand why the Roman Church, in the first flush of enthusiasm for its recent re-discovery of the Bible, should follow this path. One might have expected that the non-Roman churches, struggling to free themselves from their tradition of ultra-biblicism, would have been more cautious.

In this connection, some may feel that a valuable opportunity has been so far lost in the failure of any of the current liturgical commissions or committees to provide for the optional use of non-biblical readings in the liturgy, along the lines suggested by Christopher Campling in his two volumes entitled *The Fourth Lesson in the Daily Office* (Darton, Longman & Todd 1973–4). It has been objected that this might give the impression that such readings have equal authority with the Bible itself. The objection is difficult to sustain, since they would be on a temporary (perhaps annually) changing basis. There would be no more cause to attribute to them canonical authority than to the sermon. It might, on the other hand, tend to remove the impression that the inspiration of the Holy Spirit came to an end with the closing of the canon of scripture, and so help to fill in that arid 'desert' between the biblical writings and the present day.

2. We have noticed that biblical scholars are at one in insisting that the Bible needs very sensitive treatment and interpretation. Passages have to be seen within their proper context before they can be related to different circumstances. The quoting of isolated texts, or the conflation of texts from different settings, is a dangerous game to play both on theological and pastoral grounds. Yet it has to be admitted that a great many modern liturgies consist of little more than a catena of such texts loosely strung together, and clumsily assimilated, or rather unassimilated, to the main flow of the liturgy as a whole. Nor has there been much attempt to distinguish between biblical symbols and allusions which are still living and vivid, and those which have faded and are therefore (for the present at least) not helpful. Four examples may be given:

(*a*) At the giving of the Pax in Series 3 the President, abruptly and without explanation, addresses the congregation thus:

We are the Body of Christ. In the one Spirit we were all baptized into one body...

Now these words are wrested from their context in Pauline passages of a closely wrought, and highly symbolic kind, with a rich background in contemporary thought and imagery. The clumsy use of snippets from these passages makes of them an unattractive compound of arrogance and mystification.

(*b*) The post-communion seasonal sentence for a Saints Day in Series 3 runs thus:

You have come to Mount Zion, to God the Judge of all, to the spirits of just men made perfect, and to Jesus the mediator of the new covenant.

Now what is the man in the pew to make of such a jumble of obscure and faded imagery, unless indeed he has just read a learned commentary on the Epistle to the Hebrews?

(c) In the same liturgy, the short congregational prayer immediately following the communion of the people makes this abrupt beginning:

Almighty God, we thank you for feeding us with the body and blood of your Son Jesus Christ . . .

There is no further explanation, just this bald, sudden statement. It is indeed true that John 6 uses direct language of eating the flesh and drinking the blood of the Son of Man (language, be it noted, which is not characteristic of other New Testament allusions to the Lord's Supper), but it occurs in the context of a carefully worked out discourse which admits of no literalistic interpretation. But it is hardly surprising that its isolated and wholly insensitive use in the Series 3 liturgy should suggest to the minds of many some very highly offensive notions of cannibalism.

(d) A fourth example of this 'pepper-pot' use of biblical texts comes in the Offertory section of the Series 3 rite. Here, as the bread and the wine are brought to the Holy Table, this sentence is set for optional use:

Yours, Lord, is the greatness, the power, the glory, the splendour, and the majesty; for everything in heaven and on earth is yours.
All things come from you, and of your own do we give you.

These words of course are those attributed to King David when he asked God to accept the offering of himself and the people for the building of the Temple which Solomon his son was to complete. The words are not altogether inappropriate. But they form yet another example of the revisers' preference for bald scriptural quotation (out of context) to the composition of a prayer which will more directly and elegantly express the significance of what is being done. How much more effective are the prayers provided in the new Roman rite at this point:

Blessed are you, Lord, God of all creation.
Through your goodness we have this bread to offer,
which earth has given and human hands have made.
It will become for us the bread of life.

Blessed are you, Lord, God of all creation.
Through your goodness we have this wine to offer,
fruit of the vine and work of human hands.
It will become our spiritual drink.

Here we have two carefully composed prayers which really help the congregation to an understanding of the sacramental action, and how much better that is than peppering them with biblical grape-shot.

It may be noted in passing that the same charge cannot be laid at Cranmer's door, in spite of his concern to make the liturgy thoroughly biblical. In his services the biblical material is fully assimilated into the structure and style of the liturgy, and into its underlying theological pattern, in such a way that it does not clumsily obtrude.

3. The general effect of modern biblical studies has made it difficult, some would say impossible, to make a direct identification between the Word of God and the written words of the Bible. Yet this seems to be encouraged in some features of the new rites. In the Series 3 communion, as in the new Roman mass, there is a rubric which encourages the reader of the Old Testament lesson and of the Epistle to finish the reading with the words 'This is the word of the Lord'. To this the congregation obligingly replies 'Thanks be to God'. The older and more modest formula 'Here endeth the Epistle' had the merit of not committing anybody to any particular view of biblical inspiration. Of course one can attempt to justify the new formula by interpreting it in a broad sense. The Archdeacon of Durham has this to say: '"This is the Word of the Lord" does not mean that the words through which we hear the Word are infallible or that they cannot be bettered, it *does* mean that we should take these words very seriously indeed because God once used them to speak to a people and he has used them time and time again to speak afresh to men in succeeding centuries.'[3] But this simply will not do, for three reasons. First it is too sophisticated, and does not remove the obvious impression

that the words used are indeed infallible utterances come down straight from heaven. Secondly because it is untrue to identify words of e.g. Jeremiah or Paul directly with words which God once used. Even when words are directly attributed to God (e.g. in the giving of the Law), it is a logical and theological blunder of the first order to take such an attribution literally. The words themselves are the words of men. Thirdly, even on a high doctrine of biblical inspiration it is a false theology to identify any particular portion of the scriptures with the Word of God. The Bible in its entirety, understood as a progressive revelation of God's purposes, may perhaps be so described, but not any one part of it. The fact must be faced that some passages from the epistles contain words of Paul written in haste, and in moments of unreflective exasperation. To equate them directly with the Word of the Lord is misleading to the point of error. I cannot at this point forbear repeating the story of a conversation I once had with a very devout old lady, when we were arguing about some subject, the exact nature of which I have forgotten. Feeling myself getting the worse of the argument, I frantically made appeal to some words of St Paul. 'Ah, yes,' said the old lady, 'but that's where Paul and I disagree.' Her instinct, I feel, was more healthy and helpful than the sophisticated mental antics of many theologians.

On the same point, it does seem ironic that in many revisions of the eucharist great care is taken not to make a direct, one-to-one, identification of the consecrated bread and wine with the body and blood of Christ. Thus the 'epiclesis' in Series 3 (following the Roman canon) contains the words 'grant that by the power of your Spirit these gifts of bread and wine may be *to us* his body and his blood' (my italics). The Series 2 words of administration 'The Body of Christ' have become in Series 3 'The Body of Christ keep you in eternal life'. Presumably the motive in both cases is to avoid the impression that the bread and wine are to be identified without qualification with the body and blood of Christ. Yet there is no such scruple about making a direct identification of certain words of scripture with the Word of God. The reader may think I am making very heavy weather over just one rubric and sentence, but I think it has alarming implications. Superstition about the Word can be just as damaging as superstition about the sacrament, and at the present time presents the greater danger to the church.

4. Another general conclusion of modern biblical studies has been that in many of the biblical books, and especially in the gospels, there is a close admixture of historical statement and theological interpretation, with the latter sometimes predominating over the former, as in the Fourth Gospel. Nor is it possible to be sure that the authors to which many of the books are attributed were in fact the true authors of those books. Here again the liturgical revisers make no allowance for this, and often seem quite wantonly and unnecessarily to ignore it. A good example is the 'Comfortable Words' of the 1662 communion service. The first two of these, 'Come unto me...' and 'God so loved the world...', are attributed in the text of the office to Christ. The third ('This is a true saying...') is attributed to St Paul, and the fourth ('If any man sin, we have an advocate with the Father...') to St John. In Cranmer's day there was no reason to think otherwise. We now have reason to think that in all four cases the attribution is almost certainly false. It is therefore disappointing to find that in Series 2 and 3 the highly questionable attribution is allowed to stand. No impoverishment of the liturgy would have been involved if the words had been used without the attribution. In the new Series 3 Baptism service the 'gaffe' is even more pronounced. Here the priest says to the people, 'But in the gospel Jesus tells us that we who are born of earthly parents need to be born again, for he said "Flesh can give birth only to flesh; it is spirit that gives birth to spirit."' But there is no good reason to suppose that these words, coming as they do from the Fourth Gospel, were the words of Jesus. Then the priest goes on to say 'Baptism is the sign and seal of this new birth. Jesus commanded his disciples to preach the gospel to all nations and to baptize men everywhere.' But the allusion is to the final verses of Matthew's gospel which virtually all scholars regard as secondary; and for a number of very good reasons no scholar of repute would confidently assert that Jesus ever gave a direct command to preach the gospel to all nations, or even to baptize. It is impossible to make any sense of the ensuing controversies in the church if he had. Then the priest goes on further to say 'we read of St Peter preaching in these words...' and there follows an extract from one of Peter's speeches recorded

in Acts. But again we now know quite well that the speeches which the author of Acts puts on the lips of his characters cannot with safety be taken as a record of their actual words, but are more likely to reflect the convention of ancient historians, whereby they composed speeches themselves and then attributed them to their characters as being the kind of thing they might have said, or the kind of things which might help the historian to interpret the history he is recording. The case is worse than with the Comfortable Words, where the gospel sayings are attributed to 'our Saviour Christ'. This *could* be taken to refer to the words of the Risen Lord speaking to his church through the Spirit. But in the case of the baptism service the words are definitely attributed to Jesus in blatant defiance of the weight of the historical evidence. It provides yet another example of the lack of sensitivity shown by the revisers to the impact of biblical scholarship.

I fear that at this point I may be losing the sympathy of my readers. 'All this', I hear you say, 'is very donnish stuff, mere hair-splitting, of no interest to the ordinary man in the pew.' Perhaps, but it ought to be of interest to the minister conducting the service if he is being obedient to his ordination promise to be 'diligent in reading of the holy scriptures, and in such studies as help to the knowledge of the same'. If he is, he will know that he is making statements in public worship which the great majority of present-day devout and learned scholars of the scriptures consider highly questionable. So his intellectual integrity is at stake. The dilemma which is forced upon him may cause him to keep his studies and his prayers in watertight compartments, and will do nothing to help fill the gap between his own understanding of the scriptures and that of the congregation which he serves. Thus the gulf between the scholar and the layman will be yet widened.

But I must remind you that I write as one who believes that we must make the most of what we have got, or are getting, and not take refuge in the past. So I end this chapter on a more positive note, by suggesting ways in which some of the faults and deficiencies of the new liturgies, in relation to the use of scriptures, may be minimized or overcome. What follows is a number of practical 'tips'. They are confined to the use of Series 3, because that is the service which I know best and habitually use, but they may be relevant to other revised liturgies. It is possible, by making full use of the rubrics, many of which are permissive or optional, to make the service significantly different from what otherwise it might be.

1. There need be no more than two lessons. The gospel reading is rightly mandatory, but the other may be either from the Old Testament or read for the epistle.

2. Hymns, or other musical items (anything from a motet of Palestrina or Messaien to a pop song sung to a guitar) may be substituted for the psalms or canticles. Normally one psalm or canticle is quite sufficient for any one service.

3. It is possible on appropriate occasions to substitute a non-biblical reading, perhaps from a modern author, for the sermon.

4. In order to facilitate the preaching of a topical sermon not directly related to the set biblical readings, it is possible to separate the sermon from the reading of the gospel by a short time of silence, or by an organ improvisation.

5. The optional seasonal sentences may be used with great discretion, and the less helpful ones regularly and unashamedly omitted.

6. A determined effort may be made not to allow the sermon to become just one more part of an excessively biblical service; to avoid the hieratic tones of the liturgy itself; to be sparing in biblical allusions; to begin 'where people are' rather than with 'the world of the Bible'; above all to be warmly human in manner and approach. The same may be said of the welcome which may accompany the introductory greeting, and of the notices which may go with it.

7. In churches where there is a floating rather than a regular congregation, as in cathedrals and indeed in an increasing number of parish churches, a home-made lectionary (for weekdays as well as Sundays) may be concocted. This suggestion is meant to apply to Mattins or Evensong rather than the eucharist, when the new lectionaries are by and large more appropriate. The main principle of selection of passages should be that they are in themselves reasonably self-contained and in themselves worth hearing, rather than that they should be continuous with the days before and after. It really is quite absurdly unhelpful to submit the occasional worshipper at cathedral or college Evensong to an account of one

of the more obscure battles of the Maccabees, or one of the muddier and involved passages from an epistle, for no better reason than that it forms part of a sequence. The clergy can get their 'lectio continua' at the morning office, or through their own private biblical studies. It is high time that the relics of monastic discipline for the clergy should no longer be allowed to take precedence over the spiritual needs of the laity.

4

Worship and Theology

In the last chapter we considered the impact upon liturgy of the new approach to the interpretation of the Bible, occasioned by the rise of critical scholarship. We now turn to look at the wider field of Christian doctrine, theological understanding and spiritual experience – while recognizing that both sets of considerations interact at many points. For this reason it is necessary to reiterate the caveat mentioned in the last chapter about the in-built conservatism of public liturgy. Any liturgy which simply reflected the current fashion of theological thought, or was too closely allied to the contribution of any one theologian or group of theologians, would be ephemeral and inadequate. The preservation of continuity in spiritual experience is an important function of liturgy. So, too, is its concern to provide a vehicle of worship which Christians of widely different temperaments and religious experience may use in common. There can be no clean break with the past. Nor can there be a successful liturgy which makes no appeal to the conservative-minded worshipper.

On this score there can certainly be no genuine complaints. In spite of the changes, in spite of the superficial modernities which shock some people, the new liturgies are conservative to a fault in all essentials. Certainly there is no absence of consideration for conservative opinion in Series 3. Those with fundamentalist leanings will be satisfied by the rubric which allows the reader of the lesson to conclude with 'This is the word of the Lord'. Puritan feeling is met by the inclusion (albeit optional) of the Ten Commandments. The susceptibilities of people who object to any idea of a 'moment' of consecration, or of consecration by formula, are met by the omission of all manual acts during the recitation of the narrative of the Last Supper. Low churchmen who dislike anything which savours of the 'sacrifice of the mass'

34

will be happy that the explicit offering of bread and cup, contained in the first version of Series 2 (and in all the primitive liturgies which have come down to us), has been omitted in all subsequent revisions. Those with Adventist leanings, or who make much of traditional eschatology, must be well content by the substitution of the words 'we look for his coming in glory' for the less explicit 'we look for the coming of his kingdom' as in Series 2. The Catholic-minded proponent of credal orthodoxy will be satisfied that, not only is the Nicene Creed mandatory on Sundays and greater Holy Days, but is also virtually repeated a second time in the first part of the eucharistic prayer.

This concern to provide a liturgy which the more conservative and traditional churchman will find acceptable is to be commended. But it needs to be balanced by a real attempt also to make the liturgy reflect 'the best understanding of God in the church of the present'. This understanding has been affected by enormous advances in human knowledge, and equally vast changes in the human condition, which make the in-fighting between the various parties in the church look rather insignificant. One thinks of the revolution in human thought brought about by recent discoveries in the field of physics, biology, astronomy, psychology, and the behavioural sciences. Then there is the advent of modern technology and medicine, resulting in the emergence of a very different kind of human being, with expectations, presuppositions, and experience of life in many ways (though not in all) radically different from those of his forebears. Then there are the enormous social and cultural changes to consider – the break-up of older authoritarian structures in political, industrial and family life; the replacement of a predominantly agricultural by a primarily urban society; the mobility of populations; the shrinking of the world to the proportions of a 'global village'; problems of the environment and of over-population; the emancipation of women; great changes in sexual attitudes occasioned by the spread of contraceptive techniques; the discoveries of modern psycho-sexual studies, and a generally more permissive attitude. The list is endless. All these changes in the field of human knowledge and social patterns have profoundly affected the course of Christian understanding in the past two centuries. Much water has passed under the bridges since

Hippolytus composed his liturgy, much more since Cranmer put pen to paper. The last two hundred years have produced a whole procession of great theologians who have wrestled to re-interpret or re-formulate Christian doctrine in the light of all these changes. It will be said that the 'man in the pew' has probably never heard of Schleiermacher, Bultmann, Tillich or Moltmann. But he is just as aware as they of what it feels like to live in the world of today. And the clergy (it is to be hoped!) have been influenced by men such as these, so that some of their thinking must have rubbed off amongst the faithful. And there are some modern thinkers, notably Teilhard de Chardin, whose influence has been wider. Nor should we forget the furore occasioned by the publication of *Honest to God*, or the no-holds-barred type of TV discussion, which has exposed lay Christians to the cold blasts of theological debate from which the clergy can no longer protect them. Even if no difficulties are felt at a conscious and intellectual level, the great social and cultural changes since the scientific and technological revolutions are bound to affect the way in which the traditional formulations of the faith, and even more its symbolic expressions, are 'felt' and 'work'. The words are the same, their meaning and impact must be different. To take an obvious but much neglected example, the phrase 'Kingdom of God' must have a rather different 'feel' in an age when kings and queens are little more than figureheads (and few and far between at that), from what it had in the days of Solomon, Herod the Great, or the Tudor monarchs.

The developments in human thought and culture just referred to have had both a negative and a positive impact upon Christian understanding. Negatively they have served to challenge some, perhaps all the traditional formulations of the Christian faith, and the relevance of much of its symbolic apparatus. Positively they have served to contribute to our understanding of these formulations and symbols, expanding our horizons, giving new depth, suggesting new modes of expression. There has been both challenge and achievement.

So far we have been speaking in generalities. It is time now to be more specific, and to have a look at some of the features which have characterized the best theological thinking of recent times. It is, of course, improper to talk of 'modern theology', for there is no such animal. There is as much diversity in theological discourse today as there was in the days when the books of the New Testament were being written, and ever since. But one can trace certain characteristics which are found in most recent theological development, and which provide the various 'systems' with what has been called a 'family likeness'.

1. We find an emphasis on God's present and continuing involvement in the world which is his creation and the object of his redeeming power. One can call this thinking immanentist, if one likes. It is, however, in no way a denial of transcendence, but it is a transcendence in immanence. The 'signals of transcendence' (to use a phrase of Peter Berger's) are to be found in the ordinary, universally available elements of present, human experience, not in the sphere of the unusual or uncanny. It is impossible to give to God a living place in one's life simply by reference to some remarkable things he is alleged to have 'done' long years ago. This again is not to deny that there have been special disclosures or manifestations of God's activity by virtue of which our present experience is affected or even controlled. It *is* to say that the way in which God is said to have 'acted' in the past (in creating the world, in calling Israel, in the life, death and risen power of Jesus Christ) is the way in which he always 'acts' and still does so today. It is necessary to place the word 'acts' in inverted commas, because only so can it be made clear that God can no longer be thought of as one who, after the fashion of a physical force, intervenes from time to time upon a universe which is wholly external to his being. If we use the symbol of God 'acting' we must do so in terms of lure or persuasion rather than of external coercion or interference. This is true of his creative as much as his redeeming work. As Teilhard has put it, 'The power of the Word Incarnate penetrates matter itself; it goes down into the deepest depth of the lower forces.'[1] If God is thus involved in the whole process of creation and redemption, it follows that in some sense God suffers. Bonhoeffer tells us that only a suffering God can help. David Jenkins goes so far as to say that 'Unless God suffers there is no God.'[2] It further follows that man, if indeed he is made in the image of God, must be a real partner with God in the whole creative process, endowed with the full freedom of responsibility.

37

2. A second characteristic of recent theological thought has been a strong tendency to understand divine revelation in terms of what Bishop Ian Ramsey liked to call 'disclosure situations' rather than in terms of certain propositions, understood as in-errant and irreformable. God is made known through certain events and experiences which, when looked at in a certain way, invite the response of faith, and open up new vision. These moments of vision have subsequently to be interpreted and communicated in propositions and/or symbols. But since both proposition and symbol are conditioned by the contemporary culture and scientific (pre-scientific?) understanding, it is im-proper to make a one-to-one equation between the 'disclosure' and the proposition or symbol through which it is expressed. It follows that no credal formulation or set of symbols, however hallowed by scripture or tradition, is ever irreformable or beyond the need for adaptation to new circumstances and ways of thought.

3. There is a growing recognition that the scriptural and credal formulations of the Christian faith stand in special need today of some kind of transposition or translation. Whereas former gener-ations of Christians did not feel the need to distinguish sharply between literal statement and symbolic or mythological ex-pression, we today *do* have this need. This is due to the fact that, within the past two hundred years or so, our presuppositions about almost every subject are so very different in many respects from those of the writers of scripture and the compilers of the Creeds. So also are many of our own expectations, problems and needs. The classical statement of the Christian faith is set in the form of a story in which God is represented as having created the world (a small, flat world, more or less bounded by the Mediterranean sea-board) some four thousand years before the coming of Christ, and all at once at a datable time. At an equally datable moment the first man (Adam) 'fell', to bring ruin on all subsequent humanity. God then called Israel to prepare the way for an equally once-for-all redemption of the sin of the first man, through the coming down from heaven (conceived of in a more or less geographical way) of his Son, to undo upon the Cross the sin of Adam. He subsequently rose physically from the grave, ascen-ded back into heaven, from whence he reigns for the relatively

short space of time expected to elapse before his datable return in glory to wind up the course of a (cosily short) human history. Now all but the most literalist of believers would have to admit that there must be some accommodation here. The whole conceptualization is set in the mould of a particular world view and time scale which broke almost immediately it was cast; for the expected consummation and speedy return of Christ failed to happen. It was broken even more seriously when it was discovered that the earth is but an infinitesimal speck in an incredibly vast universe, and that the time scale of human history must be measured in millions, not thousands of years. It was finally shattered into fragments when, as a result of Darwin's discoveries, it became impossible to believe in an historical Fall, with the result that belief in a once-for-all historical Redemption becomes more questionable. I am not suggesting that we are committed to Bultmann's particular and very radical programme of demythologization; but most would agree that the myth or 'story' needs to be so re-interpreted that it may say something meaningful in terms of our present experience and self-understanding. All the great theologians of recent times have been, and still are, at work on this task. Teilhard has attempted it by relating the traditional terms and images to a cosmic, evolutionary theory. Even so basically a conservative theologian as John Macquarrie can use this kind of language: 'Creation, reconciliation and consummation are not three successive activities of God ... The three indeed are represented successively in the narrative presentation of the Christian faith, but theologically they must be seen as three moments in God's great unitary action. Creation, reconciliation and consummation are not separate acts but only distinguishable aspects of one awe-inspiring movement of God – his love or letting-be, whereby he confers, sustains, and perfects the being of the creatures.'[3] These words may sound innocuous, or even comforting, because traditional language is used. They contain a load of dynamite all the same.

4. A fourth preoccupation of recent theological thought has concerned the doctrine that only in the name of Jesus Christ may we be saved – that is to say, the traditional claim for the uniqueness and finality of Christ, and the all-sufficiency of his saving work. Such a doctrine, in an extreme form, was understandably enough

given the very limited world outlook and time scale of first-century Christians, though even then it needed some modification in the light of certain biblical passages such as the Parable of the Sheep and the Goats. It was understandable in mediaeval Christendom, when every child born in Europe was born a Christian, and the others (Jews, Turks and infidels) were people you had nothing to do with, except to exploit, or liquidate (or occasionally convert) with a good conscience in the name of Christ. It was even understandable up to a point in the great days of Empire, when the conversion of the whole world to the Christian faith seemed a distinct possibility. Today, with our vastly increased horizons, and the coming together of the world religions, it is quite obviously in need of reformation. Many of our best theologians, especially those working on the frontiers of the world's religions, are engaged on this task. Although they differ in their approach and conclusions, almost all are agreed that the uniqueness and finality of Christ must be understood in an inclusive, not an exclusive sense. This may be expressed summarily in the statement that, though Christ *defines* the saving presence and activity of God, he does not *confine* it. Or, as Bishop Ian Ramsey put it in one of the last papers he delivered before his untimely death, 'The Christian best pictures the world's religions as bearing light of different colours while holding that all light is fulfilled in the white light of Christ.'

5. The fifth and last characteristic to which I would draw attention is the search for simplicity. As John A. Baker has written: 'To a large extent the gigantic labours of theologians down the Christian centuries have been spent on resolving problems not in the Gospel but in the complications which men have made of the Gospel.'[4] Heinz Zahrnt writes in similar vein: 'We cannot imagine that the question of God is as complicated as theologians make it. God may be concealed, and can be very profoundly concealed, but he is never complicated. The complication of our theology is in flat contradiction to divine revelation.'[5] And he goes on to insist that, if theology is to be brought down to earth, then the professional theologians must do their work in the closest relation with laymen, who by virtue of their immersion in the world of down-to-earth reality must make an indispensible contribution to the theological task, so as to

prevent it becoming airborne. Some have noticed that the work of many a so-called 'radical' theologian comes very close to the actual if inarticulate beliefs of the 'ordinary Christian'. This at any rate was the verdict of *The Times*' correspondent on religious affairs about Maurice Wiles' controversial book *The Remaking of Christian Doctrine* (SCM Press 1974).

What do we find when we examine the new liturgies with these thoughts in mind? We find that the liturgical studies which have gone to produce the new rites seem to have been carried on in isolation, not only from recent biblical studies, but from the whole field of theological thought. Modern liturgies show no more than a bowing acquaintance with either the challenges or the achievements of the theologians. What was true of the intentions of an earlier generation of liturgical scholars seems no longer to be realized. We need to take careful note of some wise words of John Macquarrie: 'I wish to assert as strongly as possible that any liturgical practice or formula is to be judged in terms of theology and spirituality, and nothing is to be either approved or rejected because it happens to be in its origin first century or late mediaeval or nineteenth or even twentieth century! One may hope that through the centuries the Holy Spirit leads the Church into an understanding of truth, on liturgy as on other matters.'[6] That is the point, no liturgical practice or formula is to be adequately assessed except in terms of theology and spirituality. In a recent symposium on the Series 3 rite, Dr John Halliburton makes the point that 'The writing of liturgical prayer, (like the painting of an icon) demands not only deep personal involvement in the life and devotion of the Christian community, but also such a *degree of sensitivity to the piety and theology of the age*, together with a broad awareness of the traditions of the past and of other contemporary traditions, that the prayer which is finally composed is not the liturgists' prayer but the Church's prayer as it is the prayer of each individual Christian' (my italics).[7] Now nobody would wish to deny the involvement of our liturgical revisers in the life and devotion of the Christian community, nor their awareness of the past and of other traditions. But it may be questioned whether they have shown a sufficient degree of 'sensitivity to the piety and theology of the age'.

One of the reasons for this impression is the preference of our new liturgists for the bare, bald statement, devoid of all embroidery. In this it may be said that they are true to the literary and artistic tendency of our time. Modern poetry is crisp, not luscious; prose is Tacitean rather than Ciceronian. The trouble with the bald statement in *liturgy* however, is that it invites a wooden and literalistic interpretation of the words that are used. The need in some way to 'translate' the highly mythological language is thus evaded. The problem is aggravated by the use of modern English. The older type of language, with all its obvious archaisms, was capable of evoking deep devotion without appearing to demand a literal application of the text at the level of intellectual understanding. It was possible to make allowances. The substitution of 'you' for 'thou' as an address to God (justified as I believe it to be) has the unfortunate side-effect of obscuring the truth that God's being is uniquely different, and that therefore all language about God must always be symbolic and never direct.

Generally speaking the new liturgies, by virtue of their close juxtapositioning of a series of bald, dogmatic statements, suggest that the Christian mystery can adequately be categorized in such fashion. The New Testament, taken as a whole, does not support such a view or procedure. Here we see rich variety. There are a number of differing christologies, sometimes in the same book, each with its own cultural hinterland and subtle overtones. The saving work of Christ is presented, again often by the same author, in terms of ideas and imagery (e.g. of sacrifice or commerce or law or victory) which have the rich interplay of a many coloured fountain, but which, taken literally and in isolation, are hard to reconcile. What is more the kind of language which is used in the New Testament and in the Creeds (the sending of the Son, the ascension into heaven, the sitting at the right hand of the Father, the coming in glory on the clouds of heaven) belongs to the discourse of story not history, of poetry not prose. It is elusive language, teasing and evocative, not to be categorized or neatly packaged. It must be taken as pointing beyond itself to a mystery and an experience which cannot be contained in or fully expressed by any set of propositions or symbols, however hallowed by use and tradition.

In view of all this, it might be expected that a modern liturgy will handle such language (and it *must* handle it) with some 'sensitivity to the piety and theology of the age' and in such a way as to 'reflect the best understanding of God in the church of the present'. It is a fascinating reflection that this is the way in which Paul gave personal and living relevance to the bare bones of the primitive preaching ('kerygma'). As C. K. Barrett has pointed out,[8] we find in his writings a remarkable blending of the mythological and the existential, in such a way that they cross-fertilize each other. Unfortunately the same cannot be said for most of our modern liturgies. Leslie Houlden puts the point with some sensitivity and directness in these words: 'Demythologizing, whether mild or severe, may indeed lead to an impoverishment of imagery. It can equally lead to a restoration of a sense of the living God by removing the opiate of an obsolete story.' Even those for whom all talk of demythologizing is like a red rag to a bull may yet agree with the same author when he writes later on 'we hardly safeguard Christian truth merely by uttering its old words, out of context and unexplained. There has been little attempt to make sure that they are used in such a way as to draw out their genuine power in a modern setting.'[9]

A good example of this lack of attempt is provided by the first half of the eucharistic prayer in Series 3, which reads as follows:

> It is not only right, it is our duty and our joy, at all times and in all places, to give you thanks and praise, holy Father, heavenly King, almighty and eternal God, through Jesus Christ, your only Son, our Lord;
> For he is your living Word; through him you have created all things from the beginning, and formed us in your own image;
> Through him you have freed us from the slavery of sin, giving him to be born as man, to die upon the cross, and to rise again for us;
> Through him you have made us a people for your own possession, exalting him to your right hand on high, and sending upon us your holy and life-giving Spirit.

There is little attempt here to draw out the 'genuine power of the words in a modern setting', only a series of dull formulizations and tiresome repetitions of the 'through him' formula. The effect is wooden, hard and prosaic. We must allow that this part of the liturgy must contain an act of praise for God's goodness in creation and redemption, but that is no reason why it should read like a grocery list or an inventory.

Happily in the various forms of the new Roman rite, and in such unofficial rites as that used by the sisters at West Malling, there is no such tendency to itemize, and so to stifle the sense of mystery. Perhaps one of the bravest attempts to invest the words with evocative power and immediate relevance is made in the revised communion service of the United Reformed Church:

> With joy we give you thanks and praise, Almighty God, source of all life and love, that we live in your world: that you are always creating and sustaining it by your power, and that you have so made us that we can know and love you, trust you and serve you. We give you thanks that you loved the world so much that you gave your only Son, so that every one who has faith in him may not die but have eternal life.
> We thank you that Jesus was born among us: that he lived our common life on earth; that he suffered and died for us; that he rose again; and that he is always present through the Holy Spirit.
> We thank you that we can live in the faith that your kingdom will come, and that in life, death and beyond death you are with us;
> Therefore with all the company of heaven, and with all your people of all places and times we proclaim your greatness and sing your praise . . .

This is an improvement on the Anglican form, but there is still some overloading. It seems a pity that, in composing the eucharistic prayer, the non-Roman revisers took the ancient liturgies as their model to the virtual exclusion of their own confessional traditions. For example, what better model could there be than the General Thanksgiving in the Book of Common Prayer?

> Almighty God, Father of all mercies, We thine unworthy servants do give thee most humble and hearty thanks for all thy goodness and loving-kindness to us, and to all men; We bless thee for our creation, preservation, and all the blessings of this life; but above all, for thine inestimable love in the redemption of the world by our Lord Jesus Christ; for the means of

grace, and for the hope of glory. And, we beseech thee, give us that due sense of all thy mercies, that our hearts may be unfeignedly thankful, and that we shew forth thy praise, not only with our lips, but in our lives; by giving up ourselves to thy service and by walking before thee in holiness and right-eousness all our days...

Here we have a prayer which contains all the ingredients for the Great Thanksgiving, while avoiding most of the snags and pitfalls just mentioned. It is a truly splendid prayer; there are no dull formulizations; it is far more than a mere pastiche of biblical or credal tit-bits. More important still, the tense is predominantly present, not past. While duly including the historic perspective, its emphasis is on the ever-present activity of God in creation, redemption and sanctification.

The real trouble with the Series 3 Thanksgiving is not so much that it is dull and prosaic, but that because of this very fact it invites a wooden and literal interpretation of the words that are used. The same objection may be levelled at the Acclamation in the midst of the eucharistic prayer in many modern liturgies:

> Christ has died:
> Christ is risen:
> Christ will come again.

These words are full of difficulties. The first statement is histori-cal, the second (at least in part) theological, and the third frankly mythological. Yet here they are, stuck together in such a way as to obscure this fact, and to invite us to take them all at the same level. And whatever are we to make of the words 'Christ will come again'? We may well welcome the restoration to the eucharist of the note of Christian hope. But the expectation of the Lord's second coming was something of an embarrassment even to some of the New Testament authors, let alone to us moderns; and was subject to a number of re-interpretations within the New Testament literature itself, most notably in the Fourth Gospel. It is possible to use such language today only in a very sophisticated way, demanding a series of rather complicated mental somer-saults. It is rather deplorable that we should be submitted to such an exhausting and distracting exercise at the very heart of the eucharistic mystery, when concentration and devotion should be at their most profound.

Another glaring example of this kind of insensitivity is to be found in the Proper Preface in the Series 3 revision set for Ascension Day, which runs:

> because in his risen body he appeared to his disciples and in their sight was taken into heaven, to reign with you in glory.

Even in Sunday School it is commonly taught that the Lord's ascension is not to be thought of as a journey upward into space. It is further generally agreed among New Testament scholars that the idea of a temporary restoration of the Risen Lord to quasi-physical conditions, followed by the ascension as a second and separable event, is to be found only in Luke–Acts, and is in no way characteristic of New Testament thought, where resurrection and ascension are presented as different aspects of the same reality. It seems a pity that the intellectual difficulties posed by the reading of the Lucan narratives should be further aggravated by inclusion in the very heart of the eucharistic action. Other biblical statements about Christ's exaltation are abundantly available.

This is but one more example of the tendency of modern liturgies to be overloaded by bare, dogmatic statements, taken in isolation and unexplained. To this charge, it will be objected that after all the Nicene Creed is just like that. But the Nicene Creed was not composed for liturgical use. It was not included in the Latin mass until the year AD 1014, and even then only on high days and holidays. Later, and as a result, it was normally sung not said. That makes a lot of difference. When sung to the music of Byrd or Stravinski, or even Stanford in B flat, the baldness of the words is offset by the evocative power of the music. A quite different impression is made when it is simply recited, especially when its clauses are virtually repeated in the eucharistic prayer. There is then a grave loss of balance, and the impression is given that the heart of Christian faith lies in intellectual assent to certain correct propositions. It has sometimes been pointed out that the Creed says nothing about loving God or neighbour. This is not for one moment to deny that the Creed has a proper place in Christian discourse, but merely to question whether the liturgy should give it such prominence. I think it was Dean Inge who said that he had difficulty about reciting the Creed in public worship, but not about singing the Te Deum. One can see what he was getting at.

So far we have been considering the problem posed by the wholly 'untranslated' use of dogmatic statements. Now we turn to the question, to what extent do the new liturgies convey the sense of the 'presentness' of God? Paradoxically this *did* come across in the unreformed mass of the Roman Catholic Church, and many an old-fashioned Anglican sung eucharist. The hushed moment of consecration, the elevation of host and chalice, accompanied by the ringing of bells and swinging of incense – all these things, so difficult to justify theologically, did have the merit of expressing the gracious presence of 'le bon Dieu' in the midst of his people. What have we been given in its place? Well, the Series 3 anaphora begins promisingly enough with the words 'The Lord is here'. What follows then is described by Leslie Houlden in words which I cannot better: 'Like its Series 2 predecessor and the ancient models, it speaks in its preface of alleged "events" of the distant past, while admittedly drawing some attention to their lasting effects. God, ages ago, created, gave liberation from sin, and brought into being a people for his own possession. But few really believe that creation is something which God *did* in some immeasurably deep past, and if they do believe that, then their faith in God the creator is gravely deficient. If Christians are thought to believe it, then in the eyes of others who may be initially disposed towards Christianity, so much the worse for them. And however much weight we place on the life and death of Jesus, the faithful believer will not be content to see "redemption" as tied exclusively to those events; it is something which he knows here and now in his present relationship with God, and to speak of it solely in past terms is to remove that vital dimension. "Creation" and "redemption" may speak of the past. But they speak equally of the setting in which we now live. Is not the recognition of this the distinctive fact about Christian existence which we need to celebrate in the Eucharist? We live now in the gracious hand of God.'[10]

While still on the subject of the 'presentness' of God, and his involvement in the whole of creation, it is difficult to resist the temptation to ask, by way of an aside, why the Anglican revisers have such a predilection for beginning so many of their prayers with the words 'Almighty God'. Without raising difficult questions about the nature of divine omnipotence, it is surely true that this phrase has been so debased by centuries of improper use that it ought to be taken out of liturgical currency, or at least used very sparingly. I can remember my old grandmother, in her fiercer moods, speaking severely of 'The Almighty' when she wanted to make her point. The words have all the wrong overtones today. It is strange that the recently much emphasized characteristic of Jesus in addressing God simply as 'Abba – Father', have not left a greater impression on the re-writing of the Anglican liturgy.

Perhaps this is the right place to make some comment about the impact upon modern liturgy of the problem presented today by the traditional doctrine of the uniqueness and finality of Christ. Since this problem has only recently begun to press itself hard home, it is not to be expected that it should as yet find positive expression in liturgy. But it is, to say the least, disturbing that the Series 3 eucharist is more fiercely and uncompromisingly christocentric than any of its predecessors. In the Thanksgiving prayer the words 'through Jesus Christ' (or their equivalents) are repeated seven times. This has prompted Canon John Drury (in his editorial in *Theology*, May 1976) to comment that this results in 'an effect inappropriately more like touching wood than rejoicing in access to God'. Certainly the classical liturgies are all christocentric, but not in any aggressive or obsessional way. In them it is simply taken for granted that Christ is the only Saviour and Mediator. By contrast the christocentrism of some modern rites is aggressive to the point of obsession. They have the air of protesting too much. Do we detect in them the last, frightened protest of a dying Christian imperialism? If so, it represents a wholly negative and inappropriate response to the challenges and opportunities presented by today's dialogue between the world's religions.

Turning now to the use of symbols and imagery in worship, we find once again that their use in the new rites is for the most part un-selective, abrupt, with little attempt to give 'resonance' to the old images, let alone to find new ones. Bishop John Taylor writes: 'We are less and less at home in the language of symbols and images. Our bent, technological rather than scientific, makes us naïve and literal, so that we ofen confuse the symbol with the thing it symbolizes; and there is no surer way than this of robbing a symbol of vital significance.'[11] Our liturgical revisers seem to be peculiarly insensitive to this refection. So many of the occasional sentences in Series 3, for example, are a farrago of faded and indigestible images ('royal priesthood', 'unfading crown of glory') just put on the plate without salt or seasoning. An exception is the newly composed post-communion prayer:

> Father of all, we give you thanks and praise, that when we were still far off you met us in your Son and brought us home. Dying and living, he declared your love, gave us grace, and opened the gate of glory. May we who share Christ's body live his risen life; we who drink his cup bring life to others; we whom the Spirit lights give light to the world. Keep us in this hope that we have grasped; so we and all your children shall be free, and the whole earth live to praise your Name; through Christ our Lord.

Whatever the merits or demerits of this prayer (and there is a touch of the sentimental about it), there is at least an attempt to make images come alive, and to introduce the contemporary theme of liberation.

To return to the main subject of this chapter, it has to be said that the concepts, and theological perspectives of the new rites are for the most part wholly traditional. They reflect little either of the challenges or the achievements of Christian thought since at least the Reformation. It might be objected that to expect such a thing is crying for the moon. Yet this is what Cranmer bravely attempted, and to some degree achieved in his day. For Cranmer was not content simply to translate the traditional language of the mass into the contemporary vernacular, but to produce a new rite which would express what was then a *new* theology, the theology of the Reformation in place of the mediaeval understanding of the mass. Both Gregory Dix and Arthur Couratin[12] argue that in the service of 1552 Cranmer deliberately and with complete success gave liturgical expression to the most radical of all Reformation doctrines of the Lord's Supper, that of the ultra-Reformer Zwingli. Be that as it may, it is undeniably true that Cranmer aimed to express a doctrine in many important respects different from that which was current and traditional. He really did attempt to be sensitive to what he believed to be 'the piety and theology of the age'. And, in spite of his own biblicism, he did attempt and largely succeeded in thoroughly assimilating the biblical ideas and allusions into the texture of the rite. What was attempted then can be attempted again. For a number of obvious reasons it is a much more difficult task today. The problems are different and more intransigent. But it is worth the trying, even if the scale has to be more cautious and modest.

The tone of this chapter, as of the one before it, has been critical. So we must remember that in many ways the new services are an improvement on the old, and there is much in them for which we may be grateful. The modest suggestions I have to offer in order to make the best use of what we have been given are much the same as at the end of the last chapter.

1. It is possible, especially in the Anglican forms, to be discriminating in the use of those sections which are for optional use. As far as the Creed is concerned, seeing that its clauses are going to be summarized later in the service, it might normally be omitted on all days when it is not mandatory.

2. It is possible to make good some of the inadequacies of the liturgical texts by the use of some good *contemporary* hymns, which *do* strive to express 'the best thought about God in the church of the present'. There are some examples in the collection entitled *100 Hymns for Today*, produced as a supplement to *Hymns Ancient and Modern*.

3. The preacher of the sermon may impose upon himself a self-denying ordinance that he will never be content simply to re-echo the hieratic tones of the liturgy. He will regard it his duty both to give resonance to the traditional language so as to bring out its living power, and at the same time to proclaim the Christian message in words which are really his own, and in a way which will stimulate reflection and widen horizons.

4. There are the opportunities afforded by the more informal atmosphere of the small group or house church situation.

5

Worship and Mystery

We turn now to consider a much more familiar criticism of the new services. They are said to be, by comparison with their predecessors, lacking in a sense of the numinous. They are accused of being unimaginative, dull, flat. Do they not fail to evoke awe and wonder before the mystery of God's being? Are they not altogether too 'matey' with God? Surely they try to domesticate him, forgetting that he is transcendent, the 'wholly other', the mystery which awakens both dread and fascination in the human heart? Some extreme Roman Catholic traditionalists feel the loss of transcendence so keenly as to impugn the orthodoxy of the 'missa normativa', and talk of a new schism is in the air. Many other Catholic Christians, who see the absurdity of this position, and who would regard themselves as progressive, nevertheless deeply resent the fact that the ancient Tridentine mass is no longer available for general use, because they value in it just that element of awe and mystery which they do not find in the new mass.

Now we must be more than a little circumspect before allowing without qualification the validity of this particular criticism. We may well agree with Rudolph Otto[1] that a sense of the 'mysterium tremendum et fascinans' is essential to a true religious experience, and that the knowledge and worship of God is far more than a matter of rational understanding. Yet it was the vocation of the great Old Testament prophets in a way to 'de-sacralize' the holiness of God, to interpret it in terms of moral purity and loving-kindness. To know God is to dispense justice to the lowly and poor (Jeremiah 22.16). In the Christian view, the God who dwells in light unapproachable is also the God who draws near, who makes himself known – and does so in terms of a human life

51

and ordinary human experience. That which awakens the deepest awe in the believer's heart is the awe-inspiring quality of the humility, compassion, and self-givenness which he sees in Christ and in Christ's blessed ones. The deliberate cultivation of a sense of the numinous in worship can be a very self-indulgent, escapist and sub-Christian activity. The 'wholly otherness' of God is not best communicated by the priest standing as far away as possible from the congregation, talking in a strangely archaic fashion, and engaging in all sorts of puzzling actions which they can neither see nor understand. The new services are not to be faulted because they convey what the Lady Julian of Norwich has called the 'homeliness' of God.

Nevertheless it is the '*beyond*' who is 'in the midst'. Any form of worship which fails to convey the 'beyondness' of God must also fail of its purpose of bringing him into the midst. For if it is not the 'beyond' who is brought near, it is not God at all, but a human construction, an idol in fact. The spiritual power of the Christian proclamation of God made man is dependent on a prior belief in the mystery of God's immensity. I use the word 'immensity', not in the sense of 'very big', but to denote the fact that God's being cannot be confined by or contained in any human formulation or human ritual. 'The Ancient of Days is a year or two old' is a poetic way of expressing the central mystery of God wholly transcendent and wholly immanent. So deep is this mystery that it must be said that the closer God draws near to us, and we to him, the further he eludes our grasp. The closer one draws to the mystery, the greater the mystery becomes. That is the paradox to which all the great mystics bear witness. It follows that any Christian act of worship, and especially the eucharist, must express this mystery of transcendence in immanence, of the beyond in the midst. It must contain that 'something more', and point to the things that pass man's understanding. It is not to be expected that every service will hold the balance in the same way. An informal celebration of Series 3, or of the shortest of the four canons of the new Roman rite, will put the emphasis on immanence. A splendid Solemn Eucharist, sung to sublime music in a great cathedral, will emphasize the transcendence. The eastward position at the eucharist speaks of God transcendent, the westward of God immanent. That is as it should be. The infinite many-sidedness of God's self-expression cannot be grasped equally at the same time. Yet no Christian act of worship can be said to be effective unless, with whatever emphasis, it conveys the sense of the mystery of God, a mystery which has to be felt along the pulse, and can never be given a precise 'meaning' in words or actions.

A similar dichotomy can be expressed by the analogy of the horizontal and the vertical. God's presence may be apprehended horizontally, that is to say, through human relationships, and in community. Or it may be apprehended vertically, through a more direct communion of the soul with God. Both ways are valid, both are attested by evidence and experience. Thus for example, Paul's image of the Body of Christ is of the horizontal kind. Here Christ is envisaged as the life-principle of a community, the members of which are linked closely and directly with each other to form one organic whole. John's image of the vine, on the other hand, is of the vertical type. Here each believer is linked individually with the Lord, just as each branch draws its life directly from the main trunk of the tree.

It follows that an effective rite will hold both emphases in some kind of balance, and so provide a suitable spiritual diet for both types of believers. Now the older rites, including the Tridentine mass and the communion service of the Book of Common Prayer, did undoubtedly convey a sense of the ineffable mystery of God, and could both be used as a vehicle for deep personal devotion to the Lord. They were far less adequate to communicate a living experience of God within the community, in the depths of human relationships, and in the midst of everyday reality. The horizontal aspect of devotion was unduly subordinated to the vertical. Very commendably the modern revisers have sought to redress the balance. Have they gone too far in the opposite direction? Many answer, yes. They fail to convey the sense of mystery, they lack the note of deep devotion. There is the feeling that something precious has been lost. This is a sentiment often voiced by those who on other grounds welcome the new services, and are thoroughly sympathetic to the cause of liturgical revision. The loss is felt by the young as well as by the middle-aged and elderly. We have now to ask what substance there is to this criticism, and to what degree it may be connected with the new rites in themselves, or with the way in which they are commonly used – or, it might be better to say, misused.

This brings us at once to the question of literary merit and poetic quality, since a sense of mystery is closely bound up with the kind of language in which it may be best expressed. Now there are many who hold the view that the language of the new rites is woefully inadequate, too flat and mediocre to provide a sufficiently potent expression of worship. This view was forcefully expressed by the Dean of Guildford in a speech he made to the General Synod of the Church of England in November 1971, in connection with the Series 3 communion service. His speech was so witty that its central section deserves to be quoted in full. After saying that he believed that the Liturgical Commission, given their terms of reference, had done as good a job as any group of people could have done, he went on:

The first reason for the impossibility of the task they were given stems from the fact – I cannot imagine anyone would deny that it is the fact – that a liturgical rite is more closely related to an epic poem or a Shakespeare play, whether in contemporary or in traditional language, than it is to a piece of straight prose. I must say again, even though it has been said before, speaking as someone who has spent over half his adult life as a professional artist and who is interested in both artistic and religious symbolism, that if there is one thing I am sure of it is that a committee, however talented its members, can never be expected to write a poem or become joint authors of a new *Hamlet*, any more than the Board of British Rail can dance *Swan Lake* at Waterloo Station in the rush hour.

The second reason for this impossibility is allied to the first and arises from the fact that we live in an age which, in comparison with many other ages in the past, is one of literary infertility and linguistic poverty. It could not be a less propitious time in which to hope for the emergence at the drop of a General Synod hat of a latter-day Cranmer, and we cannot blame the Commission that no such prodigy has appeared in the event.

The third reason is rooted in the Commission's terms of reference – to produce a liturgy in contemporary language. I am all for that. All good modern poetry is written in contemporary and never falsely archaic language. False archaisms in poetry are a sure sign that the poetry is pastiche of the first order. But despite the Commission's attempts, Series 3 is full of false archaisms, and probably in a way inevitably so. It is full of biblical phrases, biblical ideas are expressed, and archaic doctrinal ideas are reclothed in contemporary words. It is not contemporary. It has resulted, if not in the worst kind of pastiche, certainly in something which is neither literary fish, fowl nor good red herring.

So much for the impossibility of the task. I believe it was a misguided task too. Why was the Commission asked to write a new liturgy? Not simply because the old liturgy was failing to mean anything to more and more people, but more specifically because it was felt that failure could be laid at the door of the old liturgy's language. The language, it was suggested, no longer communicated, it was out of date, it put people off, and it stamped the Church as an archaic relic of the past. But what nonsense this is! In a comparable case no one is presently suggesting that Shakespeare or the Restoration dramatists are out of date, that their language no longer communicates or that the Old Vic is an archaic relic to which no one wishes to go. On the contrary, they have never been more popular, not least among young people from all sorts of backgrounds and class situations. I do not deny that more and more people seem to find formal liturgical worship incomprehensible and irrelevant, but I do deny that new liturgies framed in language of semi-contemporary prose and dubious distinction will make formal worship more significant to a single person. On the contrary, the old language is the one feature of liturgical language which is still capable of ringing bells in secular souls when those souls are in distress or crisis, as any parish priest who visits a hospital knows.[2]

Now I am sure the Dean would be the first to admit that, when he poke those words, he had at least a small part of his tongue in his heek, and deliberately overstated the case. But it is a case which has o be met. I believe that it can be met, though only partially, by hese two considerations:

It may indeed be true that we live in an age which is 'one of literary infertility and linguistic poverty'. But that in itself is no argument for not doing our best to re-express the words of the ancient liturgy in contemporary language and style, in view of the great changes in linguistic usage which have taken place over several centuries. Perhaps the language and style of this century *is*, compared with the sixteenth century, impoverished. It is still *our* language; and it is fully consonant with an incarnational religion that God should accommodate himself to the poverty of our condition.

One has to ask the further question whether the language and style of the new rites (leaving aside for the moment the important question of the use of biblical allusions) is as flat and feeble as is often alleged. There are those who claim for them real literary merit, at least within the limits of contemporary style. This case is forcefully argued, in respect of Series 3, by D. L. Frost, Fellow of St John's College, Cambridge.[3] He writes: 'The real oddity is that Series 3 Holy Communion has without any conscious artifice on the part of its authors enough of the "flowers" of rhetoric to make a sixteenth-century schoolmaster coo.' He goes on to list them: 'auxesis' or 'incrementum' ('It is not only *right*, it is our *duty* and our *joy*'); 'isocolon', or the balancing of different parts of a sentence, the parts having an equal number of syllables ('to die upon the cross and to rise again for us'); 'ploce', or repetition of key words ('May we who share Christ's risen body, live his risen *life*; we who drink his cup bring *life* to others; we whom the Spirit *lights* give *light* to the world'); 'epistrophe', or the device whereby clauses end with the same word ('We have sinned . . . in the evil we have *done*, and in the good we have not *done*'). Other examples are given, but special attention is drawn to the latter half of the Proper Thanksgiving for Passiontide:

> The tree of defeat became the tree of glory;
> and where life was lost, there life has been restored,

a passage which Mr Frost describes as a little gem, comprising 'a galaxy of rhetorical effect'.

On the question of literary merit, then, there is more than one opinion. If we really understand why it is that so many find the new services, like Series 3, so uninspiring and lacking in the sense of mystery, we can hardly attribute this simply to the language and style, but must look more deeply. The trouble lies, partly with the rites themselves, partly with the way in which they are often used. First we consider the rites themselves, and the reasons they seem often to fall short in inspirational value and devotional impact.

The first reason has already been implied in previous chapters. It concerns the unimaginative way in which biblical passages and biblical allusions are quoted or made, together with the predilection of the revisers for stringing together bald, dogmatic statements after the fashion of an inventory. This is not so much a matter of literary style as of a wooden and unsubtle handling of traditional material.

The second reason applies to the Anglican revisions only. It concerns the need to satisfy the various party interests within the Church of England, resulting in the production of liturgy by way of committee work. Michael Ramsey, while still Archbishop of Canterbury, made a weighty statement on this theme in a speech to the General Synod, a speech which deserves to be quoted almost in full:

> Writing liturgy is a fine literary art, whether it is an archaic type of liturgy or a very modern liturgy in simple language. It is an art that calls for clarity of intention, including clarity of theological intention. It involves a skill in the use of words that borders on inspiration. Those great gifts are not too common in any age of the Church and they just cannot be laid upon by setting up committees and instructing them to do certain pieces of work. One man wrote the Collect for All Saints' Day, which we have known for centuries. One man wrote the Prayer of Humble Access as we originally knew it. One man – a different man in a different decade – wrote the General Thanksgiving. None of those could possibly have been produced by a committee, with one member throwing in a clause here and another a clause there. A committee can no more write a collect than it can write a sonnet.

This creates a problem in an age when we cannot boast of a great deal of the literary talent of the partly poetic kind that is as necessary for writing really good liturgy as it is for writing poetry or any kind of prose. The gifts to which I have been referring are essentially individual gifts. Looking back on the past few years, in which a great many new services have been produced, it is remarkable to note the extent to which we have been spared the marks of the committee in prayers and services. Many prayers have been produced of a simple but good quality, in clarity and in expression. But every now and then the committee-made prayer does appear. The occasions when this has happened have been just ghastly. A great deal can be learned about ecclesiastical politics from reading the text. It is evident that this phrase was thrown in to please so-and-so, and this phrase to please someone else. I will not specify the one or two instances in which this has occurred. I expect there may be silent agreement, at least on the part of a good many members of the Synod, as to what some of those occasions were.

I think the moral is this: that in undertaking and planning a still continuing big operation of liturgical revision we should bear in mind that there are limits to which a particular group can be expected to go, and, furthermore, there are limits to what may be expected at all, within a certain span of a few years, of really good quality. We cannot order chunks of liturgy in the kind of way that we get various items from the laundry. I say this because I believe that this essential understanding of what is a literary art as well as a theological art has been somewhat lost sight of in the way in which we have set about it in our proceedings.[4]

There can be little doubt that a good deal of the clumsiness and tortuousness of expression to be found in parts of Series 3 stems from this concern to satisfy all parties, to see that all have prizes. Where this happens it is not surprising that the service lacks freshness and sparkle.

The third reason is to be found in a purist insistence that *all* parts of the liturgy without exception shall be in the modern idiom, and an unwillingness to allow any of the ancient forms to survive. As we have seen, the International Consultation on English Texts has produced a modern version of all the ancient canticles of the eucharist and of the offices. There is, to be sure, an advantage in having a version of the most familiar parts of the liturgy which all churches may use in common. But the price is great. In almost every respect the older versions are more conducive to worship. Compare, for example, these versions of a part of the 'Gloria in excelsis':

Latin: 'Laudamus te, benedicimus te, adoramus te, glorificamus te: gratias agimus tibi propter magnam gloriam tuam.'

1662 Prayer Book: 'We praise thee, we bless thee, we worship thee, we give thanks to thee for thy great glory.'

ICET: 'We worship you, we give you thanks, we praise you for your glory.'

Surely here the deliberate avoidance of the hieratic style and of the steady build up of laudatory phrases has destroyed the devotional impact of the original.

Or compare the opening words of the Te Deum:

Latin: 'Te Deum laudamus'

1662 Prayer Book: 'We praise thee, O God'

ICET: 'You are God; we praise you'

The first two versions are evocative of worship, and rich in associations. The third is brash and banal to the point of absurdity.

There really is no need to produce a radically new version of time-honoured formulae so rich in association, except to substitute a new expression here and there for words which have lost or changed their meanings over the centuries. The close juxtaposition of prayers and hymns of different periods and styles need not appear incongruous, any more than we find it incongruous to see houses of different periods in the same street, so long as they are all good of their kind. As a matter of interest it may be mentioned that in the Series 3 revision of the services of Morning and Evening Prayer, one of the canticles is the ancient eastern hymn 'O Gladsome Light', in one of its old familiar translations, using the 'Thee' and 'Thou' forms of address. The principle of a mixture of styles is thus tacitly admitted. If it is acceptable to include a hymn in its original version alongside contemporary language, why not the Magnificat and some other canticles? There is good precedent for such a mixture of styles, and indeed languages. The early Greek-speaking church deliberately retained certain Aramaic phrases because of their hallowed associations ('Abba', 'marana tha'). The Latin-speaking church continued to say or sing the Kyrie in Greek. To this day all churches without exception retain the Hebrew Hallelujah and Amen, without feeling the need to explain their 'meaning' by supplying a modern translation! If we are allowed to retain Hebrew and Greek in the liturgy, it is difficult to see why a few Elizabethan phrases should do any harm.

As for the Creed, it is interesting to note that the members of the Church of England's Doctrinal Commission have drawn attention to the great variety of approach by modern Christians to the formulizations of the historic Creeds. Some take the view that, in reciting the Creed, they are expressing allegiance to the historic and continuing life of the church, rather than giving exact assent to any past formulizations of belief, which are regarded as, in many respects, relative to the age which produced them. If this opinion grows and prevails more strongly, then it is difficult to see much advantage in producing radically modernized versions of documents which belong essentially to the age in which they were first compiled. Phrases like 'of one substance with the Father' and 'was incarnate' should be allowed to stand as a testimony to the particular thought forms of the age in which the Creeds were first promulgated.

There is the further question of the musical implications of the new ecumenical texts, since almost all of them are of parts of the liturgy intended to be sung rather than said. It has to be admitted that, at least until the present time, the new texts have had a deleterious effect on church music. It is ironic, for example, that Roman Catholics must now attend Anglican worship (in cathedrals and college chapels) if they are to hear some of the finest musical settings of the Latin text! This is a serious matter, since music is for many people a very potent means of communicating the mystery of God. A number of congregational settings have been produced for the new texts, but it cannot be said that any of them are as effective as, for example, the setting of Merbecke. They are difficult to sing with ease, and one wonders whether this is due to the fact that the words lend themselves less readily to a musical setting than their predecessors. One can recollect being present at celebrations of the new rites, which have been lively enough except for the sung sections, which have sagged heavily. A few composers have written four part choral settings to these texts, but none have made their way into the regular repertoire of church or cathedral choirs. It has been claimed that musicians find the new texts eminently singable, but there is little hard evidence for such a claim. It is indeed true that the rubrics of Series 3 allow the sung sections of the service to be according to the 1662 version, so as to enable the continued use of the familiar and ancient settings. But the 1662 text is *not* printed in the service book, a factor which is likely to discourage parishes from taking advantage of the rubric. The result may well be that scores of glorious settings from the distant and recent past will be left to gather dust in vestry cupboards.

Is it, I wonder, altogether fantastic to suggest the possibility that somebody might produce new versions which followed the syllabic structure of the old, so that the same music might be used for both. This would apply to translation of the Latin into English, and of Tudor into contemporary English. This after all is the way in which the libretto of an opera is translated from one language into another. Admittedly the results have sometimes been excruciating. But today there are quite respectable translations into English of all the familiar operas of Mozart and Wagner, Verdi and Puccini, used quite regularly by so distinguished a company as the English National Opera at the London Coliseum. Probably the idea is just a fantasy, and we have to make do with the texts which are given us. On the whole, however, I incline to the opinion that the frequent use of these texts does more harm than good. It would have been better if the ancient, time-honoured and hallowed texts, both Latin and Tudor English, had been allowed to stand alongside the contemporary English of the spoken parts of the rite. The mixture need not be incongruous.

The fourth point at which the new services fail to produce an atmosphere conducive to adoration is at the Sursum Corda. It is certainly a gain that the revised liturgies make a clear distinction between the service of the Word and the Sacrament itself. But one of the results is that the action of the eucharist beginning with the 'Lift up your hearts' has to start from cold. The singing of an offertory hymn, with all the distractions of a collection being made and taken up to the altar, does not provide a very devotional introduction to the very heart of the eucharistic mystery. One feels somehow catapulted into it. This of course has always been one of the weaknesses of the Roman mass, but formerly it was masked by the silent recitation of the canon. The liturgies of the Eastern churches lead up to the Sursum Corda by means of preliminary prayers which set the tone and prepare the worshippers. The same was true of the rite of 1662. But now, in all the modern rites, there is great abruptness at this point, and it is not easy to lift up one's heart from cold.

So far we have been considering some of the ways in which the new rites are not so effective as their predecessors in setting the right atmosphere of adoration and conveying the sense of mystery. However the *main* reason for this loss lies not so much in the rites themselves as in the way they are commonly used and handled. It is not sufficiently realized that the celebration of a revised rite, facing the people, has to be very carefully spoken and 'choreographed', if it is not to be dull or even absurd. It is all too easy to make a list of the horrors that occur. There is the priest who recites the prayers in a rapid or monotonous way, wantonly throwing away his best lines. He does not realize that, whereas the splendour of the old rites could carry him along, with the new rites he has to do the carrying. Then there is the celebrant who fiddles with his glasses in full view of the people, who does not know what to do with his hands, or who keeps kneeling down, thus providing the hilarious spectacle of a head and neck protruding above the altar-table. Sometimes the Pax is passed round a quite large congregation, taking ages to accomplish, and producing little but boredom, or embarrassment, or both. Sometimes the service begins with a long hymn, followed by the Kyrie and then the Gloria in Excelsis, so that the congregation is quite exhausted before the service proper has even begun. The time of the administration of communion is unduly prolonged through inefficient management. The service may be further elongated by the use of all the optional parts, the garrullity of the intercession leader, and a long, fussy process of 'washing up' after the communion. Often the lessons are read by laymen or laywomen (sometimes children) who are quite inexperienced in public reading or speaking, and who murder the words they speak, if indeed they are audible at all. Sometimes the children present are so fractious and noisy that attention becomes virtually impossible.

The reader may think I have painted a dark picture. But there are no grounds for despair, since many of the difficulties just mentioned can in fact be overcome. In spite of some quite serious inadequacies and infelicities, the new rites *are* capable of being presented in such a way that at least a modicum of reverence, adoration and mystery is preserved, without destroying the 'homeliness' and community feeling which are equally important. So, at the risk of seeming to lay down the law, I would like now to offer some simple suggestions of the ways in which the new services may be used to the best effect, how they may be enriched in practice, and how at least some of the inadequacies may be overcome.

1. I would like to see in every diocese regular courses provided for clergy and lay people in parishes which are embarking on one of the new rites, or who, having embarked on it, are making heavy weather of it. Such occasions would provide useful opportunities for discussing such things as the appropriate postures and gestures of the priests and ministers as they face the people across the altar; the best way to arrange the furniture; the most effective way of giving outward expression to the Pax; the pros and cons of using ordinary bread, and, if it is used, how to do so without awkwardness and distraction; how to make the most effective use of music and of silence; what recommendations to give to the congregation about standing and kneeling (the practice of standing for the first part of the eucharistic prayer and kneeling for the second half is quite contrary to the intention of the rite; it is one single prayer, and the same posture, preferably standing, should be adopted throughout); how to make the administration both reverent and expeditious (this will normally mean using laity as well as clergy); how to be sensible and business-like about the ablutions (best done in a side chapel or vestry, so that it does not hold up the action of the service). These may seem small matters, but inattention to such details has the cumulative effect of making the service heavy and tedious, thus robbing it of its power to engender the true spirit of worship.

2. If lay people are to read lessons or lead intercessions (and it is

highly desirable that they should), then they should be chosen carefully and given some instruction and guidance. If any should aspire to read or pray in the public liturgy of the church, then he or she should be willing to submit to an audition, just as he would if he wished to join a choir with high musical standards. The sole criterion for the privilege of reading at the liturgy is the gift of reading well, not being a representative of this group or that. These observations, it hardly needs saying, are meant to apply only to public and formal liturgy. On less formal occasions, as for instance in house group celebrations, there will obviously be much greater freedom and spontaneity.

3. Opportunity might well be taken to enrich the service by the use of local artistic talent, both within the congregation and on its fringes. I am referring to such things as solo singing, an instrumental interlude, an organ piece, an item performed by glee singers or a pop group, even perhaps a mime or ballet. There is much to be said for adding variety on suitable occasions by a multi-media approach. But it is essential that what is offered is good of its kind, within the compass of the performers, and such as to add something really significant and inspiring to the worship. It must not be done simply for its own sake, or just for a change.

4. Then we return to the enormously important question of music in worship. There are many for whom music is not a way to God, for God has made them tone-deaf. But there are many for whom it most certainly is. When it is bad music, or music badly performed, then it becomes a positive barrier to living worship. I am referring, not only to full-scale choral music, but also to congregational music which is badly chosen, inadequately accompanied, and beyond the range of the congregation to sing with any facility. In this matter almost everything depends on the relationship between vicar and organist, or between Dean and Chapter and Master of the Choristers. Unless they think of each other as partners in a common task, each respecting the integrity of the other in their respective though overlapping spheres, then the worship is bound to suffer accordingly. The subject of vicar-organist relationship should certainly have a place in the syllabus of theological college and first incumbency courses.

Where it is decided to use one of the congregational settings to Series 3 or related rites, then it is vital that there should be several good congregational practices before the new music is introduced, and that the same setting should be used for a good long time so that it may become thoroughly familiar. If, after all that, it still fails to 'catch on', then it should be abandoned, and an alternative given a trial. Or perhaps it might be thought better to confine the music to the hymns and psalms alone. There is nothing worse than plugging away at a setting which nobody enjoys, and which lowers the temperature of the whole service. If on the other hand a parish can boast of a good choir, then it should be allowed and encouraged to include in its repertoire, not only any new music for the revised rites which may be produced, but also the traditional settings of the unrevised texts. Mass produced and cheaply printed service sheets make possible the offering of alternative texts, or translations, side by side. It is much to be hoped that the new People's Service Book, expected to be produced for Church of England worshippers in the next few years, will contain the old and the new versions of the canticles printed in parallel columns. In the meantime parishes ought not to be discouraged from producing their own service sheets with both texts printed alongside each other.

Then there are the hymns. So often these days churches combine a revised liturgy with a totally unrevised hymnody. 'Unrevised' in this context should not be taken as a synonym for 'ancient'. The word is used to connote lack of sensitivity to the piety and religious understanding of the age, whether in words or music. This has little to do with the date of composition. The 'Vexilla Regis' ('The royal banners forward go') is ancient and excellent. The hymn 'Throned upon the aweful tree' is comparatively modern and appallingly bad. Nor is it a matter of popularity. 'Onward Christian Soldiers' and 'The Church's one Foundation' are equally popular; but the words of the former breathe the air of a discredited triumphalism, while the words of the latter are theologically sound and of contemporary significance. 'Abide with me' and 'The day thou gavest, Lord, is ended' are again equally popular. But the mawkish, self-pitying tune to the former is at odds with contemporary spirituality, while the warm, robust and lilting waltz rhythm of the latter is of enduring appeal. Some parishes have their own liturgical group or committee. It would be an excellent Lenten exercise for such a group to work steadily through the hymn book, putting on the index of forbidden hymns those which failed the test of suitability for contemporary worship. If the exercise were of sufficiently Lenten austerity, probably less than a quarter of them would survive.

5. What shall we do with the children? We do not wish to keep them away, but there is a great deal of sentimental nonsense talked in favour of keeping *all* of them there for *everything*, regardless of the sometimes intolerable degree of distraction caused to other worshippers, to say nothing of the boredom inflicted on the children themselves. There is everything to be said for a crêche for babies and tiny tots, at least for a large part of the service. If that is impossible then the little ones should be in some part of the church where there is an easily accessible escape route when disaster strikes. Nor is the very back of the church necessarily the best place for them. Somewhere quite near the front might be better, where they can see what is going on, preferably on a thickly carpeted area, and with no heavy furniture around. It is the proximity of small children and hard surfaces which causes most of the bother.

6. A list like this would not be complete without reference to the place of cathedrals in liturgical revision. The rôle of the cathedral is rapidly changing. On the one hand the cathedral is now so expensive a commodity that it needs, in present circumstances, to justify its own existence. On the other hand it is being presented with much greater opportunities as a result of the ever increasing number of people who visit it, or wish to use it. No longer may it be content simply to 'preserve the heritage of the past', a phrase which is usually taken to mean doing things as they have always been done. It must also be a pace setter, from which others may draw inspiration and ideas. The nature of the building justifies a certain grandeur and solemnity in its ceremonial and music. By the same token the sheer size of the building, with its great expanses, and also its many smaller chapels and nooks and crannies, invites a greater flexibility, and makes possible acts of worship which are more experimental or adventurous. The paradox of the cathedral is that it can become the home of worship which is both more grand and also more informal than is feasible in other types of church buildings. Both possibilities should be exploited to the full. There is no reason why a cathedral should

not present a Series 3 eucharist, celebrated with dignity but in a warm and unstuffy fashion, with plenty of congregational participation, and *still* go on using the finest musical settings from the sixteenth to the twentieth centuries. It needs a good deal of care and imagination, but it can be done and ought to be done.

Traditional cathedral Choral Evensong deserves a mention too. It is my belief that cathedral Evensong is a service which could come into its own at this present time. Culturally, it is a jewel beyond price. Spiritually it provides just the kind of reflective, unbusy, contemplative worship for which many are hungering. It is a significant reflection that, when the BBC some years ago proposed to drop the broadcasting of cathedral Evensong on the Third Programme, there was such an outcry of protest (coming in some cases from non-believers like Miss Marghanita Laski), that the BBC saw fit to change its mind. Admittedly it will appeal only to a minority, but it is today a significant minority. The fact that the service is so under-valued and poorly attended is partly the fault of the cathedrals themselves, where there may be a patronizing 'take it or leave it' attitude. Little attempt is made to make it better known or understood. Neither a warning notice at the entrance to the Quire nor a 'welcome' over the loudspeaker is likely to induce casual visitors to attend a service, but when some of them *do* respond to an unobtrusive, but friendly notice, they should be properly looked after, and the service made more approachable by a careful selection of psalms and readings. It is likely that for some time to come the 1662 service will be used for cathedral Evensong. But it is possible that, at some future date, a revised and modestly modernized version might take its place. Has any liturgical commission ever thought of undertaking such a task for specifically cathedral worship?

7. The use of music is closely linked with the use of silence. Both are potent instruments for setting an atmosphere of deep worship; both may counteract the excessive wordiness and clumsy dogmatism of the rite itself. There is no need to commend silence in worship, since its value has been established, especially among the young. On the other hand, the use of silence must be wholeheartedly and carefully planned. There is nothing more fretful than having a multitude of short pauses constantly interrupting the flow of the liturgy. The rubrics of Series 3, for example, allow

for silences in a number of places, but it is not intended that all of them should be used. It is best to have one, or at most two, periods of silence of reasonable duration. The times following the sermon, the thanksgiving, or the communion are all suitable. There are, of course, some people who, in this excessively noisy age, are oppressed by complete silence, so that there is a case for covering these periods with very quiet, unobtrusive organ improvization. Congregations could be consulted about this matter, so that each could follow the pattern it found most helpful.

In conclusion, the substance of this rather diffuse chapter may be summed up in two simple propositions. First, the intelligent and imaginative combination of the old and the new in the same service is not an anomaly but an enrichment. Secondly, whatever is done in public worship should be within the competence of the congregation, while stretching its resources to the full. Simplicity and excellence are not opposites, but complementary. Let what is done be appropriate to the resources and the occasion, but never shoddy or second-rate.

6

Creative Worship

If the contents of the last few chapters have been critical of many aspects of our revised services, it is time to remind ourselves that, given their terms of reference, and assuming the continuance of church life more or less as it has been in the past, the various committees and commissions have done their job very conscientiously. This is especially true of the Church of England's Liturgical Commission, which has produced the new services with great care and untiring energy, making good use of many of the resources at their disposal. The churches have decided that they wish to have more contemporary official acts of worship, of a basically traditional type, and the agencies to which this task has been assigned have been extremely conscientious in fulfilling it. It is no reflection on their efforts if we raise the awkward question, have events already overtaken them since they essayed their task? It is no longer so clear as once it seemed that 'bringing the liturgy to life', understood in terms of regular Sunday worship in church or chapel, is having the revitalizing effect that was expected. It would seem that the liturgy as now celebrated, in spite of the modernizations, still appears irrelevant to most young people, whose outlook on life and whose responses are formed very much by the mass media. The expectation that young people will grow into Christian maturity mainly by means of parish church type worship, and especially of holy communion, looks like being a false hope, at least for the present. This has been brought home to me most forcibly by various discussions I have had with older school children and especially sixth formers. They are by no means philistine in their approach. They can appreciate a good, thought-provoking sermon. Many of them can appreciate great religious music in church, and much resent being 'sung down to' when they are on 'church parade'. Yet the actual ritual and ceremonial seems to leave them cold. Is it because insufficient efforts are made to explain its meaning to them? Or does the cause lie deeper than that? Certainly it is a desolating experience to be present at a eucharist, in a cathedral or school chapel, where the large body of school attenders, though well behaved, seem to be joined in a tacit conspiracy of studied non-participation. On the other hand it is not too difficult to persuade youngsters to assemble in large numbers for special non-traditional 'festival' or 'celebration' types of worship; nor does it worry them if these go on for two hours or more, or even all night, so long as they feel that something is 'happening' – a feeling which they do not seem to get at regular worship. This has led some people to hold that while attempts are being made to revitalize traditional Sunday worship, the 'action' now lies elsewhere – that it lies in what Bishop Michael Ramsey has called 'experimental Christianity'.

Now one manifestation of such experimental Christianity is undoubtedly the special 'festival' or 'happening', and something more needs to be said about it here. These events are usually multi-media affairs, needing very careful rehearsing and preparation, sitting very lightly to traditional forms, involving a good deal of congregational participation (though the participants do not think of themselves as a 'congregation'), not only in words but in physical movement. Above all they have to be relaxed, unregimented, unhurried, relatively unstructured. This is not such an entirely new thing as is sometimes supposed. The great Easter night festival of the Orthodox Church in Russia and Greece has something of the same air about it. Dr J. G. Davies has discovered some fascinating things about the prevalence of dance in certain areas of the church of early times, sometimes as a ballet type 'performance', sometimes involving the congregation, at least in certain mimetic actions. Dr Jasper, now Dean of York, and Chairman of the Liturgical Commission, has also written about a number of present day experiments along these lines.[1]

It is interesting also to reflect that some of our traditional carols were written to be danced as well as sung. Ronald Knox once made the point that the traditional High Mass (now no longer found in its former complexity and complication of movement) resembled a highly stylized and stately kind of dance. A number of parish priests are finding that, in spite of the increased lay participation in the new services, there is still too little for the congregation to 'do', too little bodily movement. Some deans and provosts are wondering whether too little advantage is being taken of the vast space of the cathedral, especially when children's services are being held in them. Ought there not on such occasions to be a great deal more moving about? The popularity of some of the freer, more spontaneous forms of charismatic worship may well be due to the increased scope that is given, not only to spontaneous utterance, but to bodily movement as well. Then again one often hears of priests who, having little opportunity for celebrating the eucharist, complain bitterly about 'not having an altar'. I suspect that part at least of what they miss is the bodily movement and physical actions to which they have become so accustomed that it is now bound up very closely with their own religious experience. One wonders whether some members of our congregations, subconsciously no doubt, feel similarly deprived of any real opportunity to give outward, bodily expression to their religious emotions. Perhaps that is why new style processions and pilgrimages are becoming popular. Then there are a growing number of parishes where there take place regular 'family ser- vices', based on a theme, and using multi-media methods. These clearly serve a real need, and are often very satisfying. It is important that the church should be aware of these various essays in experimental worship, since they may be found to contribute to a more relevant form of liturgy, and perhaps come in time to have a fertilizing influence on the more regular worship of parish churches.

However, it has to be admitted that the number of such 'happenings' which could be described as successful has been rather small. Some of them are too ambitiously conceived to be workable. Some are marred by a vulgar and inauthentic element of mere gimmickry. Some fall down in that they use forms and symbols which, though in tune with contemporary ideas and values, are in fact essentially alien to the true Christian ethos and understanding. It is not here that one can detect a deeply signi- ficant growing point in the church's life. If then the 'action' is not here, and if there is reason to question whether the main 'action' is in the regular Sunday worship of the parishes, where does it truly lie? The answer which is often given is, in the life of small groups of Christians, who really know one another at a deep level, who are profoundly united in certain common and specific aims, and who are developing their own forms of worship. The rest of this chapter will be devoted to the subject of worship in small groups.

These are of very varied kinds. Some are informal cells or house churches growing out of, and forming part of, the life of a parish. Others are centred in various experiments in community living. Others are connected with common interests, as in schools, colleges, or industrial mission. Others are concerned with particular aims, 'action groups' to deal with pressing social problems in a locality, like drug addiction, alcoholism, race relations, housing, or the care of the homeless. Others again, more especially in countries under oppressive regimes, are politically motivated. All of them are increasingly ecumenical in their membership.

Now this development raises a basic issue about liturgy. For, on the one hand, it seems quite clear that no centrally devised form of liturgy is likely to be of much use to so great a variety of situations. It seems inevitable that each group will wish to evolve a liturgical pattern which directly expresses its own concerns, and which grows out of its own roots. And these are likely to be more radical than anything so far produced by any of the official bodies for general Sunday use. On the other hand, our various liturgical commissions and committees are busy devising services which will be uniform, and capable of universal use. There is here a clash between the interests of uniformity and diversity. The recent publication of the Report of the Church of England's Doctrinal Commission (called *Christian Believing*, SPCK 1976) has emphasized both the value and the inevitability of theological diversity in the church. The same must surely be true of the devotional forms in which such diversity seeks to express itself. The Chairman of the Commission writes elsewhere, 'Just as there is widespread agreement today that no one approach to theology can claim absolute priority over all others, so we ought to expect and even to welcome the same sort of variety in eucharistic thought and piety.' Having allowed that the historical link with Jesus must continue to be in some sense decisive in the development of eucharistic worship, Professor Wiles goes on to say: 'But even if this is what is decisive, might not the eucharist still be able to draw more widely than it does upon the varied forms of corporate activity which are natural to human societies? If, for example, the eucharist is intended to provide an expression and experience of joy and fellowship, it might seem that in our contemporary culture dancing and relaxed conversation over a drink are the most natural ways in which to make that provision. Within the liturgy there are admittedly words and actions intended to fulfil this role, but their conventional form often prevents the effective communication of these realities to us ... The central act with the bread and wine in association with Jesus is irreplaceable if the sacramental action is to retain its distinctively Christian meaning, but there may well be scope for its linking with a broader complex of other forms of sacramental action.'[2]

Professor Wiles might agree with me that, in this last sentence, it might have been better if he had substituted the plural 'meanings' for the singular 'meaning'. It has always been the case that in the eucharist there has existed a rich variety of 'meanings', a vast range of spiritual experience and symbolism in the rite, so rich and vast as to defy precise definition or codification. Even in the past the eucharist has 'meant' different things to different people within the same tradition. The present situation in regard to biblical interpretation only serves to accentuate the diversity of meaning; for it is recognized that the 'meaning' of biblical texts has to be re-interpreted in the light of new knowledge and fresh ways of experiencing the reality of the world in which we live. When you add to this the great variety of the Christian cells and groups which we are discussing, it becomes all the more unlikely that any one form of eucharist will be equally 'meaningful' to them all. It is as misleading to speak of the meaning of the eucharist as it is to speak of the meaning of *Measure for Measure*, or of a Beethoven symphony or quartet.

One way to sum up the matter is by saying that there are two approaches to the problem of worship today. One is the way of liturgical revision, undertaken centrally and imposed upon the people. The other is the way of liturgical creativity, in which new forms are thrown up from within the fellowship of local Christian (usually ecumenical) groups.[3] It is important to realize that, although the approach of revision makes the headlines, and has the greater initial impact upon the largest number of Christians, the approach of creativity is just as valid, and may possibly be of more lasting significance in the life and development of the church.

Before looking a little more closely at what is already going on in small group worship, it must first be freely admitted that the development we have been discussing is subject to certain inevitable limitations, lest we run away with the idea that the informal liturgies of small groups are the answer to all our problems. First, there is the danger that such groups, in their liturgy-making, will succeed in expressing only themselves, and their inevitably limited Christian experience and understanding; whereas it is a function of liturgy to bring Christians to an understanding of God and his ways which is wider and better than that which they already hold. Secondly, it would be generally admitted that any celebration of the eucharist worth the name must express both the transcendence and the immanence of God. It is almost inevitable that any particular celebration will put the emphasis on one or the other, and it is unreasonable to expect that every celebration should keep them in exactly even balance. But there is the danger that some forms of highly informal celebrations will so emphasize the immanence as totally to obscure the transcendence. The fellowship of the Spirit can and does sometimes degenerate into a very earth-bound and worldly kind of matiness. Paul appears to have faced some such problem in dealing with the goings-on in the Corinthian house churches of his day. Thirdly, there is the danger of élitism in this small group worship. For example, the Ashram Community, no doubt, has an important part to play in the total life of the church, and for some will fulfil a spiritual need which they fail to find in the life of the institutional churches. But one cannot but feel distinctly uneasy when one reads that the members of its annual conference in 1971 wrote of it in this way: 'The Ashram Community is a group who no longer see the institutional church to be doing the Jesus thing, except marginally here and there, and are searching to bring together meaningful units of people who can "be the Body of Christ" in a thoroughly secular way ... The Ashram Community is 1. The only Christian alternative for today's church. 2. Tomorrow's church in today's time. 3. The living church within the community...'[4] Such statements seem to ignore the lessons of church history, where the search for

74

the 'perfect church' or the 'community of the elect' has always come to grief. It looks rather like a modern version of Montanism or Donatism, or similar movements which turned out not to have much future.

So a cautionary note has to be sounded. Nevertheless the fact that informal, creative liturgy is subject to certain limitations and dangers does not mean that it is without value; far from it. In fact it is very much on the increase at present. It is to be found amongst conservative evangelicals, whose traditional prayer meetings nowadays sometimes end with an informal celebration of the Lord's Supper. In the series of Grove Booklets on Ministry and Worship, there is an interesting issue by Derek D. Billings,[5] in which seven unofficial texts of the eucharist are offered for the use of small group worship. Some of these texts are longer and relatively traditional. Others are very short indeed, and owe little to traditional forms except for their biblical language.

Then there are the charismatic types. In his sensitive little book *The Charismatic Prayer Group* (Hodder & Stoughton 1975), John Gunstone devotes a chapter to describing how a charismatic group may celebrate the eucharist informally in somebody's home. He states that to try to reproduce a church service in a domestic setting is artificial, and that something more informal is required. He then goes on to suggest ways in which such informality may be obtained, and how spontaneous singing, or speaking with tongues, may be integrated into the worship. It is, however, interesting to notice that Mr Gunstone, himself a loyal Anglican, does not recommend extempore prayer for the eucharist itself, nor even the use of unofficial texts as presented in the Grove Booklet just mentioned. Instead he suggests either Series 3, with certain abbreviations, or one of the prayers authorized for trial use by the Episcopal Church of the USA. He writes: 'To gather round an ordinary table in a home and to hear the prayer of thanksgiving which they normally hear on Sunday mornings said over an ordinary plate and a cup gives them deeper insights into the nature of the Church's eucharistic celebrations.' Certainly Mr Gunstone has a point here. However, there is another aspect to this question to which we will turn later. It should also be noted that charismatic groups less attached to the traditional churches than those of which Mr Gunstone writes exercise considerably

75

greater freedom in the way they celebrate the Lord's Supper.

Next we ought to mention the informal worship which has been going on amongst certain Christian groups which are politically inspired, or even revolutionary in their aims. There is, for example, the so-called 'Underground Church', a movement which arose within the Catholic communion in the USA, its members consisting of those who have become disenchanted with the Roman Church's apparent failure to implement the promises of the Second Vatican Council, and who are also intensely concerned with social and political action. It combines informality, left-wing political commitment and a radical kind of immanentist theology. Because its members are largely derived from the Roman Catholic or Episcopalian Churches, the eucharist is central to its meetings. At present the movement is on the wane, but its worshipping life has been often creative and adventurous in its form and content. In an article on this subject, John A. Cooke writes: 'One finds in the Underground Church a breakdown of old dichotomies. There are home-grown liturgies in city after city; men, Catholic and Protestant, are writing baptism services for their own children; couples are composing marriage services; these to be held in home settings; yet the Underground is not withdrawing from the world, but embracing it ... In the worship of the Underground, the songs, the language, the gestures, the food and drink are all taken from contemporary life. Compared with the Mass one might feel that the element of mystery is missing, but the point is made that one might be able to discern the real meaning of mystery and of faith. Faith is no longer related to another world but to the mysterious in this world ... It does not attempt, or pretend, to be inclusive or balanced, indeed it cannot be because so much of it is the worship of protest against both the Church as an institution and society at large. But this liturgical experience, whatever its shortcomings, carved out of the commitment to live on the frontiers of theology and political involvement, will be ignored by the Church to its cost.'[6]

This is a very brief and incomplete account of some of the things that are going on in the realm of what we have called creative liturgy. Some of it is impressive, some alarming. My own trouble with it is that it is not creative enough, and that for three reasons. First, it tends to be confined to certain groups which are in one way or another extreme, and whose members have very strong convictions of a particular kind, theological and/or political, which are not shared by the majority. That is fair enough. But we have already noted that no one theological position is likely to be able to claim absolute pre-eminence in an increasingly pluriform church. What about all the people who do not subscribe to any of these extreme positions? Secondly, although the worship of the evangelical or charismatic type is informal enough, yet when it comes to the heart of the eucharist, and of the central prayer, these groups tend to be timid and not especially creative. In the charismatic group worship recommended by Mr Gunstone there is a deliberate avoidance of any deviation from the official norms at this point. The seven eucharistic texts presented in the Grove Booklet above mentioned, although informal in style, are in fact tightly bound up in the language and imagery of the Bible. In any case, to take an unofficial instead of an official form for regular use is hardly creative. It does not grow in any way from within the group itself. It is no less imposed from outside simply by being an unofficial production. Thirdly, and most importantly, liturgical freedom seems so often to go hand in hand with rigidity in doctrine. Informality is allied with fundamentalism. A flexible practice accompanies an inflexible theology. On one of the BBC's religious programmes called *Sunday* recently a young man was asked what he valued about the charismatic type worship which he constantly attended. He replied at once 'Freedom – you are free to do *anything* – you can testify, you can sing, you can speak with tongues – you can do what you like – except, of course, you've got to keep the doctrine as it's given over.' That is to say, you can *do* anything in worship, but you are certainly not allowed to *think* anything. In the creative liturgy of many of these groups we have been considering, the problems raised in chapters 3 and 4 of this book are simply not faced at all, indeed they are not recognized as problems.

So there is the very real danger that creative liturgy will become the preserve of ultra-conservative or extremist groups. This is a serious matter, because the church today needs in liturgy, as in all else, the full participation of its 'central' or 'liberal' members. These are the people who are unwilling to accept any party badge, who cannot avoid asking the awkward question, who care about truth even when it is uncomfortable, who are searching for a faith to live by, and who indeed are well on the way to finding it, but who cannot without loss of integrity subscribe to some of the given dogmas in their present forms. Should they not be given the freedom to explore and experiment in corporate worship like the others? Should they not be more anxious to do so? There is today a serious danger that the resurgence of conservative or irrationalist forms of spiritual renewal will leave the 'seekers' out in the cold. Thus the door of the church may be closed on some of the most perceptive and sensitive Christians and potential Christians in the world today. Thus renewal and enthusiasm, whose reality I would not wish to deny, will have been purchased at a heavy price.

So what is the answer to the problem? How is liturgical creativity to be encouraged among small, informal groups of Christians, who are aware or are becoming aware of one of the central dilemmas of liturgy still largely ignored. I refer to the dilemma that, in finding a living and relevant liturgy for our times, either in general or for special purposes, the greatest single problem is posed by the Bible itself. For no amount of modernization of the liturgy, however skilful, can remove the inescapable archaisms of the biblical readings and allusions. To put it another way, the central dilemma is that the words which are used have either changed their meaning or lost their meaning. Experience shows that it is not very likely that the official revisions will get very far in solving this dilemma; in some ways they have made it worse. So one looks to the small group of worshippers to do some pioneering work in this field. This most certainly does *not* mean that we need a welter of unofficial forms to be produced for their use. It is to be hoped that we shall not follow the example of the Episcopal Church of the USA in producing a number of alternative 'canons' for the use of house celebrations. The suggestion now being made that the Church of England's Liturgical Commission should produce such forms will, I trust, be resisted. Such a procedure, essentially bureaucratic as it is, stifles rather than assists true creativity. There have been times when I have myself attended small, ecumenical house group meetings, where there has been a high degree of freedom in discussion, a sharing in depth of hopes and anxieties, and an establishing of real community in the real world. The eucharist has followed with a great sense of expectancy. But somehow, when the little copies of Series 3, or whatever, have been passed round, and the service begun, there has been a sense of let-down, of disappointment. An atmosphere of comparative unreality has replaced the very real, here-and-nowness of the group meeting; and a feeling of slightly embarrassed restriction has supervened upon the very great spontaneity and naturalness of what had preceded.

What appears to be lacking on such occasions is a form of celebration which really matches and expresses the experiences and insights which the group has gained, and thus has its roots in the living situation. What is required is greater freedom, a freedom which will include the option to use or not to use material from traditional or ancient sources. One such 'home-grown' liturgy is the well known rite as prepared for the people and clergy of St Mark's-in-the-Bowerie, New York. One chapter of John Robinson's *But that I can't believe* (Fontana 1967) is devoted to this subject and contains the text of the liturgy. It was very much a common project (involving W. H. Auden who was a member of the parish at the time), and took many months of preparation. The result is a service which has great freshness and directness. None the less some of the nettles have not been fully grasped. John Robinson, in spite of his enthusiasm has this to say: 'It has not really tackled what I am sure cannot be put off much longer in liturgy or hymnody, a serious attempt to reckon with the question Bultmann has raised in theology. "O Father, who sent your only son into the world to walk among us, as a man, upon our earth" still makes Jesus like a being from another planet who was, astonishingly, really human. How to re-write this would be an interesting subject for competition – for those who feel the difficulty. Those who do not need not enter.'

Yes, but some *do* feel this difficulty, and one does not need to think in terms of competitions! Progress could be made if the groups, who are seeking a form of eucharistic (or non-eucharistic) worship which meets their condition, were encouraged to be more adventurous, more free from inhibitions, and prepared to improvise more than they do. Those with any knowledge of the history of the liturgy will recognize that this would not be something new, indeed it would be a return to something very old. We know from the evidence of Justin Martyr, who wrote in the early part of the second century, that, before set rites for the eucharist had been formed, the president improvised his own Thanksgiving, or eucharistic prayer. It is thought likely by some that some of our earliest surviving liturgies, as for example the Apostolic Tradition of Hippolytus, comprise a kind of outline for improvization, and may be transcripts of the spontaneous prayer of some especially talented celebrant. Much later on, the solidification of liturgies into set forms did not prevent adventurous churches, in Spain and Northern Europe, from producing their own versions, with a great profusion of imaginative, even riotous, elaboration. Pentecostalism, together with some of the sects, have a tradition of spontaneity in eucharistic worship within a broad framework. So what is here being suggested has plenty of precedents. It may have been wise for the church of an earlier age to cut back such luxuriant, and sometimes superstitious, growth. No doubt it is still wise to seek a measure of uniformity in the rites used regularly in parish churches. But circumstances have changed. The growing acceptance of a measure of variety and pluriformity in doctrine and worship may best be expressed by allowing and encouraging a greater freedom and adventurousness at the level of the house church or small group.

This is certainly not to say that such indigenous liturgy must be in 'everyday language' or be unconcerned about style. Some of the group members might well possess literary or poetic gifts which could be used to advantage. On the other hand there would be no need for such liturgies to be enduring, or capable of universal use. They need last for no longer than the groups which have produced them survive. The vital thing is that they should fulfil the real needs of the group out of which they have grown, and that their production should help the group towards a more mature understanding of what its members are doing, or seeking to do, when they worship together.

What might this mean in practice, as far as the eucharist is concerned? It would mean that official encouragement should be given, not only to liturgical revision, but also to liturgical creativity, in small groups and on informal occasions. This aim could be achieved by a policy of turning a blind eye, and perhaps that is how it is already working out. But it would be better if creative liturgy were officially recognized, encouraged, and thus delivered from the dangers of sectarianism. All that then would be required would be the issuing by the bishops, or other church authorities, of a set of certain basic and mandatory rubrics or directives. They would be very short, and might run something like this:

1. The president shall take bread and wine, with or without words.
2. The president shall give thanks for God's goodness and mercies, making the memorial of Christ, and including in his prayer one of the New Testament narratives of the Last Supper. He shall pray in his own words, or in words chosen by him, or in words agreed upon by the group.
3. The president shall break the bread, with or without words.
4. Those present shall eat the bread, and drink of the cup.
5. Any embellishments by way of ceremonial, bodily gestures, use of music etc. shall be at the discretion of the group.

Nothing more than this is required to constitute a valid eucharist, except some directives, where appropriate, about the ministerial orders of the president, and the baptismal and communicant status of the participants. Anything more than this would inhibit the freedom and creativity which is to be desired.

7

The Prospects for Worship

Where do we go from here?

The brief and somewhat diffuse reflections contained in this book have, I fear, presented a confused and confusing picture. But if they have, it mirrors faithfully the realities of the present situation. It might also be said that I face two ways, and to this charge I freely admit. So do many other worshippers at this time of rapid change, confusion and experiment. There is much to be welcomed in the new services. But it is an insidious temptation to imagine that, once the present round of revisions is over, and Series 3 (and her sisters) finally take over, we have reached our journey's end, and can begin once again to talk about 'our incomparable prayer book'. We must, however, venture some sort of opinion on what may be the way ahead. Where do we go from here in the matter of liturgical worship?

Some would say, 'Nowhere. We have reached a dead end. The liturgical movement has run out of steam. People are wearied by it all. The attempt to bring Sunday worship alive must be declared a failure. In short, Sunday worship, as ordinarily understood, has had its day.' That is possible. But I see no cause yet to be so deeply pessimistic. The need for some kind of celebration or liturgy is deeply embedded in human society. Where its religious forms have collapsed, or been suppressed, secular substitutes (of a much less attractive kind) have tended to emerge, as for example in communist China. One of the disadvantages of our western pluralist societies is their lack of any kind of significant celebrative occasion to give cohesion and express common ideals. This need for some common liturgical expression must be all the greater in such a society as the Christian church, with its proud claim to be both catholic (i.e. universal in its scope and appeal) and apostolic (i.e. with deep roots in tradition and a real continuity through past, present and future).

So we can reasonably count on the drive towards liturgy endemic both in human society in general, and in the church in particular. Nevertheless it can hardly be denied that at the present time, and for some time to come, there is and will be a serious tension between what I have called the principle of liturgical revision and that of liturgical creativity, between the formal and the experimental.

Some would, therefore, argue that, though we need not run to the extremes of pessimism, we must expect a time of considerable confusion, and emerging from it, in all probability, a much greater regionalism in liturgy. We must expect a return to the days described in the preface to the prayer book when 'there hath been great diversity in saying and singing in churches within this realm; some following Salisbury use, some Hereford use, and some the use of Bangor, some of York, some of Lincoln...' Only today the diversity of use may be expected to be much more extensive. Perhaps every parish will, in effect, have its own 'use', its own particular variation on the common forms, its own liturgical commission. To some extent this is already beginning to happen, and it has its healthy and promising side to it. But the prospect of extreme regionalism, with every parish having declared a kind of liturgical UDI, is a depressing one. It would make the worst of both worlds. We would lose the advantage of a familiar liturgy universally available in each denomination, with common features immediately and easily recognizable. We should lose the almost priceless advantage of not being at the mercy of the parish priest or minister – or perhaps the local Reader. We should lose the advantage of knowing what to expect when going to worship. These are all advantages which the process of liturgical revision seeks to preserve. On the other hand we should also lose, or tend to lose, the opportunities for genuinely free, adventurous creative liturgy, since the public worship of church or chapel is not a fertile breeding ground for that. So there would be no compensations, but rather the opposite. Extreme parochial regionalism is no answer. It would result in even greater confusion and no less mediocrity than at present.

My own modest and tentative proposal, for what it may be

worth, is that the way ahead lies in, not one, but two directions; and that these need to be followed simultaneously, and with equal enthusiasm.

First of all, we now need a new prayer book for each denomination. By a prayer book I mean an officially authorized book which may be found in the pew and in the home. This would contain all the main acts of public worship, both regular and occasional. It would represent the conclusion of the present stage of liturgical revision, and make use of its best fruits. It would not this time be expected to have a life of several centuries, but only of, say, one or two decades. That is to say, its life might be measured by the time when the first printed and bound copies begin to wear out! Some churches have such a book. At the beginning of 1975 the Roman Catholic Church in this country published (only semi-officially, I understand) an 800-page Sunday missal for popular use, and well over 100,000 copies were sold in ten months. In October of that same year the Methodist Church published a 256-page service book, and this too is proving popular. Other churches are doing, or have done, something of the same kind. The latest news from the Church of England is that, at the February session of the General Synod in 1976, a Report from a Working Party under the chairmanship of the Bishop of Durham was presented on the subject of a proposed alternative service book. By a substantial majority the Synod voted to accept the main proposal contained in this Report. This was to the effect that the Church of England should publish an officially authorized People's Service Book, containing a full range of alternative services, but excluding everything which is already to be found in the 1662 Book of Common Prayer. It would include all the main services, bound together under one cover. The present Series 3 services, after some further revision and tidying up, would form the major part of its contents. It might be expected to appear in about 1980, and to have a life of ten years at the least. It could not be called *the* prayer book of the church of England, because the 1662 book would continue to be published and legally available for use. However, the Church of England may now reasonably expect that by about 1980 it will have, in effect if not in law, a new prayer book replacing the plethora of little booklets currently in use. This is a development which I believe is to be welcomed.

That may seem an unexpected judgment in view of the highly critical comments which have been made about the new liturgical forms, and especially Series 3. But liturgical revision, like politics, concerns the art of the possible. It seems clear that, given the present climate of opinion in the church, we cannot for some time expect anything very different from the current forms, though we may still hope for some last minute improvements. If the hope is not realized, then we must make do with what we have got, and comfort ourselves with the thought that the admitted inadequacies and infelicities of the current forms may be set against the real advantages of possessing once again a prayer book to be found in the pew and in the home. These advantages are considerable. The authors of the Report to the General Synod, just referred to, sum the matter up well in these words: 'With a book of this kind, the church member can prepare for a service, follow it in his own book in church, and have it available whenever he wants it. This was the norm before the present programme of liturgical revision, and was an immense spiritual advantage ... A book of the kind we propose with, say, an expected life of at least ten years, could help to provide the stable setting which has traditionally been needed for the full development of Anglican spirituality.' Admittedly the thought of the 'missa normativa', Series 3, and their sisters, as the staple liturgical diet in our lifetime (I write as one of the older generation) is not one which can be greeted with much enthusiasm. But the alternatives are still less attractive, and there is always the hope that our children will have something better when the time comes.

This hope, however, will be realized only if the church is bold enough to follow simultaneously a second and contrary course. This is the positive and willing encouragement of the utmost freedom and creativity in liturgical expression as suggested in the last chapter. This kind of creative liturgy, springing from within rather than imposed from outside, will be found in small groups of various kinds, and whereas regular, public liturgy will continue for the time at least, to take as its starting point the rehearsing of God's revelatory 'acts' as set out in the scriptures, the liturgy of the small group will tend to be centred in present concerns, to take the world of the present as its starting point, and to be more 'thematic' in character. There will be here a shift of emphasis

85

from the past to the present, without denying the necessity of dialogue between them. It is, however, of the utmost importance that these local, experimental forms of liturgy should be allowed to develop in freedom, without the necessity of being tied down by any traditional or authorized forms, though use may be made of them. Where the eucharist is concerned, the only measure of episcopal control should be the minimum suggested in the last chapter.

So I end by expressing a modest hope. If both these courses are pursued together, with equal enthusiasm, and with the life line open between them both, then there is at least the possibility that their interaction will fructify and enrich each other. Those who engage in creative liturgy may be preserved from undue subjectivism, eccentricity and sectarianism by virtue of their exposure to the authorized forms of public worship, now enshrined in a proper Prayer Book. Conversely the insights gained by experimental worship may serve to enliven acts of public worship, and lead later on to the production of another prayer book for the twenty-first century which will reflect more adequately changes and advances in spirituality and theological understanding, and be better adapted to contemporary needs and aspirations.

So let public worship continue to be in accordance with forms duly revised and authorized. But let there be a return to the days of Justin Martyr in the conduct and development of liturgy at small group level. Let both proceed together. Let both be equally acceptable. Let both be seen to be equally conducive to the church's health and vitality.

Notes

Chapter 1

1. A. G. Hebert, *Liturgy and Society*, Faber 1935, p. 8.

Chapter 2

1. *Theology*, Vol. LXXVIII, No. 658, April 1975.
2. Trevor Beeson, *The Church of England in Crisis*, Davis-Poynter 1973, pp. 88–9.

Chapter 3

1. See D. E. Nineham, *New Testament Interpretation in an Historical Age*, Athlone Press 1976.
2. *Theology*, Vol. LX, No. 450, January 1957.
3. Michael Perry, *Sharing in One Bread*, SPCK 1973, pp. 24–5.

Chapter 4

1. Teilhard de Chardin, *Le Milieu Divin*, Fontana 1964, p. 61.
2. David E. Jenkins, *The Glory of Man*, SCM Press 1967, p. 107.
3. John Macquarrie, *Principles of Christian Theology*, SCM Press, Revised Edition 1977, p. 269.
4. John Austin Baker, *The Foolishness of God*, Darton, Longman & Todd 1970, p. 400.
5. Heinz Zahrnt, *What Kind of God?*, SCM Press 1971, p. 129.
6. John Macquarrie, *Paths in Spirituality*, SCM Press 1972, p. 78.
7. *The Eucharist Today* ed. R. C. D. Jasper, SPCK 1974, p. 95.
8. C. K. Barrett, *From First Adam to Last*, A. & C. Black 1962, pp. 83–91.
9. *The Eucharist Today*, p. 172.
10. Ibid., pp. 172–3.
11. John V. Taylor, *The Go-Between God*, SCM Press 1972, p. 238.
12. Gregory Dix, *The Shape of the Liturgy*, Dacre Press 1945, ch. 16. Arthur Couratin, *The Service of Holy Communion*, SPCK 1963.

Chapter 5

1. Rudolf Otto, *The Idea of the Holy*, OUP 1923.

2. General Synod, Autumn Group of Sessions, 1971, Report of Proceedings, Vol. II, No. 3, CIO 1971, pp. 626–7.

3. *The Eucharist Today*, ch. 10.

4. General Synod, July Group of Sessions, 1973, Report of Proceedings, Vol. LV, No. 2, CIO 1973, pp. 354–5.

Chapter 6

1. In an article contributed to a symposium entitled *Worship and Dance*, published by the Institute for the Study of Worship and Religious Architecture, University of Birmingham 1975.

2. *Thinking about the Eucharist* Essays by members of the Archbishops' Commission on Christian Doctrine, SCM Press 1972, p. 116.

3. See J. G. Davies in The Research Bulletin of the Institute for the Study of Worship and Religious Architecture, University of Birmingham 1972, p. 5.

4. Quoted in J. J. Vincent, *The Jesus Thing*, Epworth Press 1973, p. 69.

5. Derek D. Billings, *Alternative Eucharistic Prayers*, Grove Books 1973.

6. Research Bulletin 1972, p. 8.